ROAD TO DAMASCUS

A Journey of Faith

WYATT TEE WALKER

MARTIN LUTHER KING FELLOWS PRESS® NEW YORK

LK

FOREWORD BY JESSE JACKSON

Road To Damascus

Copyright 1985

Martin Luther King Fellows Press, New York, N.Y. 10026

Library of Congress Cataloging in Publication Data

Walker, Wyatt Tee
  Road to Damascus
Includes index and appendix
1. United States-foreign relations. — Syria.
2. Syria-foreign relations-United States.   3. Goodman,
Robert O.   4. Walker, Wyatt Tee. 5. Jackson,
Jesse-Journey to Syria-Damascus I. Title
E183.8395W35   327.7005691   84-29477

ISBN 0-937644-03-X

Designed by Ray Leonardo & Jules Wagner
Front cover design: Jules Wagner
Photo Editor: Theresa Ann Walker
Typeset by Daryl Lindholm
Printed and bound by Leonardo Printing, Mount Vernon, N.Y.

To Jim Conte

DEDICATION

To my wife and sweetheart
of thirty-five years,
THERESA ANN WALKER
and
the entire congregation of
THE CANAAN BAPTIST CHURCH OF CHRIST
in New York City's Harlem

Best Wishes

Wyatt Tee Walker

Other Books by Wyatt Tee Walker

THE BLACK CHURCH LOOKS AT THE BI-CENTENNIAL

SOMEBODY'S CALLING MY NAME

CHINA DIARY

THE SOUL OF BLACK WORSHIP

COMMON THIEVES*

*For release Spring 1985

Author's Preface

This work has been a labor of love. I studiously kept careful notes during my stay in Syria because I suspected the historic significance of our mission. The release of Lt. Robert O. Goodman a year ago today certified my suspicion. Upon my return to the United States, I immediately wrote a two thousand word essay about the last moments of this fantastic adventure. It was part of a publisher's kit (outline of proposed book, chapter titles, sample chapter, etc.) that my literary agent shopped around. Not only did we not interest any publisher, major or minor, we could not get a nibble for even a magazine piece on this extraordinary event in American foreign affairs. We both felt we had to strike while the iron was hot but all our efforts ended on a publishing dead end street.

Sorely disappointed, I set my notes aside. Over this past summer, it occurred to me that the people who make history, seldom have a hand in writing history. I decided for the sake of an accurate record, I owed it to Mr. Jackson, the Afro-American community and our allies in the struggle for peace and justice to complete this work. In the middle of October, I earnestly set about the task of making permanent the record of what really happened on the road to Damascus.

I am grateful to Dr. M. William Howard whose constant encouragement kept me at this task. During the preparation of the manuscript, my personal secretary was felled by serious illness and I enlisted the help of another Canaan parishioner with great stenographic skills, Ms. Elsie Jefferson. Ms. Jefferson met every deadline with punctuality and good humor. I am indebted to my pastoral assistant, the Rev. Carolyn Knight and my bride of thirty-four years, Ann Walker, who proofread the original manuscript. A second kudos is due M. William Howard for the critical reading of the final galleys to insure the accuracy of my personal recollections of events, times and places. Especially am I grateful to Julia Jones who supplied a selection of photographs that helped to fill the gaps of my personal photographic record. One of Ms. Jones photographs was chosen for the cover. For the second time within a year, the Martin Luther King Press, Inc. has allowed me the use of its imprimatur to make this record permanent. Special thanks are due the members of my academic society and its president, Dr. Henry H. Mitchell.

Lastly, the Canaan congregation deserves some special mention for its generosity in continually sharing me with the community and the world. We should all be thankful that the good Lord is working as He is in the life and spirit of the 'Country Preacher', the Rev. Jesse Louis Jackson.

Wyatt Tee Walker
New York, N.Y.
January 3, 1985

An Introduction
by M. William Howard, Jr.

I shall always remember the feeling of relief I felt upon arriving at Kennedy Airport that cold December 27th evening in 1979. My two colleagues and I had just returned from conducting Christmas services for the U.S. Embassy personnel being held hostage in Iran, and this experience had been undoubtedly one of the high moments of my ministry. But, as far as I was concerned, it was the kind of high moment you only wanted to experience *once*. So I quietly promised myself that I had had enough of international intrigue for awhile — in fact, forever!

That promise lasted until December 19th in Memphis, Tennessee last year when Jesse Jackson raised the prospect of appealing to the Syrians to release Navy pilot Lt. Robert O. Goodman. Now, I realize in a way that I may never have in quite the same way what my grandmother meant when she used to say, ". . . when the spirit moves." In this book, Wyatt T. Walker tells how the spirit moved.

This journey of faith made an indelible mark on all of us, not because of its obvious drama, but largely because of the bonds of friendship which the ordeal cemented among the participants, no matter their particular roles.

If you followed the events that led up to and followed this mission with keen interest, you will want to read this book closely. Keep in mind that this is the first insider's account of what happened, and it may be the only one to be written. And it is so fitting that Wyatt should be our historian, since he is himself a kind of "living thread" which runs through the Afro-American's modern-day struggle for justice and peace. He was Chief-of-Staff for Martin Luther King, Jr. during the tumultuous, yet productive, Birmingham Campaign. And in more recent years, he has traveled extensively as a preacher and as a promoter of international understanding.

The author is a man of unusual "at-homeness" among people of other cultures; he has an uncommon capacity to enjoy life and to delightfully "embellish" his considerable talents without embarrassment or without taking himself too seriously. He is also firmly planted in the Black church tradition, which colored and informed — from beginning to end — the assumptions, the style, the arguments and even the audacity which comprised the attempt to win Goodman's freedom.

The Black Church's unyielding, literal belief that God can / will / does intervene in history was ever-present in the Syrian mission, as Walker's account reveals. The book also tells how the journey originated and unfolded, thus putting to rest the sometimes reckless speculation of the press.

There can be no doubt about the seriousness of the mission or the seriousness of thought which went into its preparation after reading *Road to Damascus*. And as it is with any mission of such gravity, there are also memorable and touching moments; moments of downright fun! And my good friend Wyatt would never miss anything as robust and as consequential as tears of joy or a good belly laugh.

Finally, through the whole tour I kept seeing the genius of the African experience at work — regretting through this and most of my growing international experience how America has failed so miserably to use this great natural resource effectively, to help solve international crises. There is something in the suffering of the ex-slave which lends itself to cultivating understanding among peoples of vastly diverse backgrounds. I have seen this with my own eyes in so many, many settings.

I think here of that marvelous Afro-American diplomat who played such a pivotal role in resolving the Iran hostage crisis as Ambassador to Algeria. Or I think of Paul Robeson, who did more than any other single man to put "Apartheid" into America's vocabulary over thirty years ago. The list of such stellar achievements is long but all-too-often suppressed. This is not to be chauvinistic, but just to think about it and wonder how things would be if they were otherwise.

Keep this in mind when you read Dr. Walker's bitter-sweet account of our historic journey of faith.

December 12, 1983
Princeton, New Jersey

The Rev. Jesse Louis Jackson

Foreword

Road to Damascus is an important book. It may well be one of the most important books of this or any year. This book does far more than provide an historical account of our faith-mission to Syria that resulted in the release of Lt. Robert O. Goodman. It provides in microcosm the context of how we shall come to a new world order. More than anything else, it certifies my firm belief and that of others, that there is an alternative to war and armed conflict. The "no-talk" methodology of U.S. foreign policy is neither philosophically sound nor pragmatically prudent. If we do not talk, we will not act; if we do not act, we cannot change. We must talk!

This record of our Damascus experience details how nations and individuals in adversary relationship may differ geo-politically but in dialogue rise above provincial and nationalistic interests to demonstrate the higher demands of faith and morality. We need to talk! The explosive exigencies of the Middle East, the obscenity of South Africa's apartheid, the military quagmire of Central America and the enigma of Afghanistan are all within the nuclear purview of the superpowers. This reality demands that we talk. There is another way. My mentor and leader, Martin Luther King Jr. was quite correct in asserting that allegiance to the Hammurabic Code of "an eye for an eye" will leave too many people blind.

Wyatt Walker, Harlem's renaissance man, has provided a faithful and faith-filled narrative that is honest and lucid. He possesses the gift of many Black preachers — he is a great story-teller. He makes the reader see and feel our faith. With sensitivity, he lays bare our humanity and is never too pious to note our laughing and crying. Every devotee of our common sturggle for peace and justice should read this book. It is an affirmation of our faith in the future.

Jesse Louis Jackson
Chicago, Illinois,
January 1, 1985

Table of Contents

List of Figures

Photo Credits

Cover photo: Julia Jones.

Photo opposite Foreword, courtesy of Jesse Jackson For President Committee.

Julia Jones, pages, 21, 36, 50, 71 (bottom), 78, 87, 111, 113, 114, 117, 119, 120, 122, 125, 129, 131

Akbar Muhammad, page 45.

All others, Wyatt Tee Walker.

PROLOGUE: The Big Moment

Tuesday, January 3, 1984

As I walked across the hotel lobby my counterpart and new friend, Syrian Chief of Protocol, Khalil Abu Hadad asked, *Can Reverend Jackson be in the Foreign Secretary's Office at 10 o'clock?*

Let me run upstairs and see, I responded with outward calm. My heart began to race. At the third floor landing, I vaulted out of my brass cage like Carl Lewis out of the starting blocks for the hundred yard dash. I zipped past the command post of the U.S. Embassy staff without a glance. A member of the Secret Service detail who was very familiar with my normal "cool," called to me, *What's up, Reverend?,* as I continued on to 367, Jesse Jackson's suite. The agent at the door was already turning the key. In I burst, my face lit up like a Christmas tree. The sliding door to Rev. Jackson's bedroom was to my right. I stepped in and pulled the door almost closed. Jesse Louis Jackson looked up, not startled but not casually, either. He had been immersed in reading one of the several documents that Tom Porter, his chief campaign aide, prepared each day.

Leader, I began conspiratorially, *can you be in the Foreign Secretary's office at ten?*

His eyes widened and he shot back, *If I need to be!* He was wide awake but still in his skivvies.

You need to be! I said confidentially and with the air that this was it. The Biggie!

Immediately, the country preacher from Greenville, South Carolina began to dress.

This was almost a complete reversal from what the Syrians had outlined the night before. Monday night, after several hours of waiting for the promised answer to Goodman's fate from Syrian's President Assad, Mr.

1

Jackson had receive an official request to delay our departure to the U.S. A firm promise was made through Assad's office that a "high Syrian Official" would bring us the President's decision by 10:00 a.m.

The pace since our arrival was either dizzying or maddening; too fast or too slow. We left New York with three assurances in hand from the Syrian Ambassador to the U.S.: a meeting with religious leaders of Syria, a visit with Goodman and an audience "with a high Syrian official."

On this Tuesday morning in Damascus, the plane with our fifty-four cancelled seats, was half-way to Frankfurt and we were sitting in the Foreign Secretary's office. Earlier when I reported to Hadad that Mr. Jackson would be available at ten, he took me aside and said confidentially, almost conspiratorially, that *I think you ought to go this morning.*

I retraced my steps to Jesse Jackson's suite to clear my presence in the meeting with him. He was fully dressed now. The brothers on Lenox Avenue would have said, "Clean as the Board of Health."

My throat was dry and my heart was pulsating like the sound of a runaway freight train. The photo opportunity for the media was at an end. The small talk between Abdel Halim Khaddam, Foreign Secretary of Syria and the Country Preacher, Jesse Louis Jackson, had awkwardly run out. It was 10:11 a.m. The atmosphere in the Foreign Secretary's office was tense, electric.

Mr. Jackson, the official interpreter began, *The meeting this morning will be a brief one.*

The decision had been made. I thought to myself, this is it! For some inexplicable reason I had always been optimistic. I kept telling the others, *Don't worry, the Lord is in it.* I was convinced I had seen

2

God working in Jesse's life in much the same manner that I had seen Him working in Martin Luther King's twenty years earlier.

The interpreter continued . . . *President Assad has asked me to inform you that on the basis of your moral appeal* . . .

I WAS READY TO SCREAM!

. . . *we shall release to you Lt. Goodman.*

For a millisecond, this scenario seemed unreal. The American press and a large segment of the American public including some critical Blacks, were poised, expecting Jesse to fall on his face. The most improbable players in this international drama were a country preacher from Greenville, South Carolina and an alleged strong-armed Arab dictator. In this single instant, it seemed Jesse Jackson had accomplished the impossible.

At the precise moment that the interpreter finished that brief statement, Jesse Jackson shot up from his chair as if a hot poker had been put to his posterior. For a split-second, he seemed transfixed in disbelief. Then he grabbed Khaddam and in Oriental fashion, kissed him on both cheeks. Quickly he called for a prayer of thanksgiving. Fervently in traditional but diplomatic tone he thanked God for helping to "break the cycle of pain." In irreverent fashion, I peeked at our circle of prayer and I saw the foreign secretary's eyes glisten with tears. I was crying too.

At 11:30 a.m, January 3, 1984 just a little more than an hour later, Lt. Robert O. Goodman was a free man.

The narrative that follows is the behind-the-scenes events that led to this moment from the December 19th meeting in Memphis, Tennessee when the idea was first discussed, through the intricate preparation

3

for the trip, the discussions in Damascus, and Goodman's release.

Along the way, many of the public myths and press accounts that surround the mission will be shattered. This mission was never a certainty, and it was not embarked upon for political purposes. Above all else, it was a journey of faith, a mission of earnest believers seeking to inject religious tenets into a war torn situation.

How It All Began

Memphis, Tennessee and Damascus, Syria are worlds apart geographically and culturally. Memphis is a big sleepy town astride the Mississippi, fabled in American folklore for cotton, southern belles, W.C. Handy and Elvis Presley. It is the most unseemly place for the beginning of an international drama. Yet it was in Memphis, at the Holiday Inn, Riverside that the journey of the Rev. Jesse Louis Jackson to Damascus, Syria began. On December 19, 1983, "the Country Preacher" was holding court in his twelfth floor suite while an unseasonable blizzard vented its fury on the city.

His rapt audience was a tight knot of activist Black clergy who had come to Memphis for a one-day Summit Conference of Black Religious Leaders to consider the proposition of Jesse Jackson for President. Its attendance and agenda was in utter disarray because of the blizzard. A city-wide mass meeting had fallen victim to the weather also. Jackson was trying to salvage something from the effort and time expended.

I don't know whether you know it or not, Jackson said in his patented confident style, *but there's a Black navy flier who's a prisoner of war in Syria and the United States has forgotten about him.* The South Carolina born and bred country preacher continued, *The Washington Post reported last Saturday that Donald Rumsfeld met twice with the Foreign Secretary of Syria and never mentioned Goodman's name.* He jabbed the air with his right hand for emphasis.

I mused to myself, *I wonder what Jesse's got in mind this time.*

The Country Preacher continued, *I took it upon myself to send a cable to Assad asking for Goodman's release on humanitarian grounds since its Christmas time and all that. I have no idea what his reaction will be.* The PUSH leader went on. *I do think that if a delegation of high profile religious leaders would go to Syria, we may be able to get them to turn him loose.*

As is his style, Jesse Jackson looked straight ahead into the eyes of Bill Howard and said,

Bill Howard, I want you to head this mission. It must be ecumenical in make-up if it is to have the proper impact.

In the assembled group of about twenty-five clergy-men and high echelon staff, I was standing to his left at the outer perimeter of the circle. The Country Preacher's eyes searched the room like an eagle searching it's prey. His gaze riveted on me and as swiftly as he had picked the chairman for this mission he said to me, *Wyatt, you need to make this trip.*

After singling out another two or three persons in the room, Jesse Louis Jackson admitted this was a tough time for pastors to leave their responsibilities but this was a matter well worth the sacrifice. The room was buzzing with the anticipation of how this whole situation might develop. Jackson surmising that the trial balloon of his suggestion was a success, mentioned almost apologetically, that each person joining the mission would bear their own expense. The excitement in the room became more subdued after that remark.

In my own mind, even though Jesse had mentioned me by name, I couldn't see how I could make this trip at Christmas. As the main discussion broke into smaller groups, Bill Howard button-holed me and reminded me that the celebration of Christmas in the Eastern churches was around January 6th or 7th. I thought to myself "Maybe I can make it after all.

The overwhelming consensus was that this was a tremendous idea and should generate broad support.

Some home phone numbers were hastily exchanged and a couple of us extracted from Jesse Jackson's aides the best notion of where he might be for the next several days. There was much to be done and we needed to have immediate access to him.

Before the session broke up for the evening, Jesse reminded us that he was scheduled to appear on Good Morning America and would launch the "blue ribbon" campaign. We had agreed that we would all wear blue ribbons until Goodman was released. This was part of our consciouness-raising campaign around the Goodman issue. All of us committed ourselves to push the campaign from our pulpits on Sunday.

Early the next morning, we said our good-byes and enplaned for various points around the nation.

Thursday, mid-day, December 22nd, when I arrived·at my church office, C.T. Vivian was on the phone. C.T. and I are old friends from the King days* and was now doing the national staff work for the Church and Clergy division of Jesse's presidential campaign. He was calling to confirm my participation in the mission to Syria and advise me of a change in the proposed date. The ecumenical delegation was now scheduled to leave for Damascus on December 27th, a week earlier than suggested in Memphis. Originally the departure date was set for the Wednesday *after New Year's* and now it was being moved to the Wednesday *before New Year's*.

I told C.T. I was committed to the proposition but that in light of this new development I needed

---

*Author was Chief of Staff to Martin Luther King Jr., 1960-1964.

twenty-four hours to give it some thought. In my heart, I desperately wanted to go but I wanted a chance to talk with my wife Ann, and the Chairman of the Board of Canaan and my Pastoral Assistant on whom the burden of my absence at Christmas would surely fall. This was a tough time for a pastor to be away from his congregation.

By noon Friday, my decision had been made. It was accelerated by a call from Jesse early that same morning. He told me he had in hand a cable from President Assad, personally inviting him and a delegation of his choice to Damascus. This was obviously in response to Jackson's cable a few days earlier.

It is imperative that we put together a prestigious delegation he said, and intimated that in light of this personal invitation, he was seriously entertaining the notion of interrupting his campaign and joining the delegation.

It's really that important!

At the time I wasn't sure whether he was trying to convince me or himself, or both of us. Fortunately, I had already talked with Mrs. Walker, Chairman Elmo Cooper of Canaan's Joint Board and The Reverend Carolyn Ann Knight; all were agreeably disposed to the importance of this mission in spite of the holiday. I told the Country Preacher I was ready to "get on the Damascus Road" and to keep me posted. I did not realize at the time how prophetic that jocular rejoinder would be.

My wife and I were married on Christmas Eve, so on this our thirty-third anniversary, we spent most of the day together in Manhattan as we had done every year since the children were grown. Just about dusk, we made our way back to Yonkers. The phone was ringing as we came in the front door.

I betcha' that's Jesse I said. It was.

Where have you been all day! I'm sick of calling you, Harlem Preacher! I quickly explained the anniversary thing and he just as quickly withdrew his friendly tirade about me being so hard to reach.

Jesse Jackson frequently makes a statement which is immediately followed by a question which in light of the statement can only be rhetorical.

Wyatt, Chuck Percy has arranged a State Department briefing on our trip to Syria. It's at 2:00 p.m. Monday (This is Saturday, Christmas Eve). *I need you to be there. You have to be there! Can you make it buddy!*

Ann pieced together what was going on and I could hear her muttering with some unhappiness, *Good Lord! That's the day after Christmas!*

When I hung up the phone, it was settled; I would catch the noon shuttle to Washington on Monday, meet Jesse and other members of the mission who could make it at the Howard Inn and go to Foggy Bottom in a group.

Within a few minutes, Bill Howard was on the wire, anxious to know if I had spoken to "the Candidate." I told him I had and we would be seeing each other on Monday.

Right! he said, *However, there's a more pressing matter now. Our proposed delegation is an all Black delegation at the moment and as important as it is to be ecumenical, it's equally important for it to be interracial.*

I really didn't agree but there were no grounds for me to resist his thesis. I thought it would be nice if we could get some high-profile white preachers to go, but in my view, it wasn't crucial. (I was mistaken.) Howard's next thrust caught me off-guard.

9

Wyatt, while I'm confirming the rest of the mission, I need you to make a couple of calls to see if we can't make it interracial too.

Look Bill, I responded, *I just can't give any more time to Damascus tonight; let me get through my Sunday services and I'll give it a shot.* My mind was racing ahead. *What white preacher do I know who would consider going at Christmas?*

Who comes to mind? Howard asked, interrupting my thought.

I weakly replied that we certainly ought to start with Bill Coffin. William Sloan Coffin, an ex-CIA man and now a somewhat controversial minister of the Riverside Church, had been arrested with me during the Freedom Ride when he was Yale University's Chaplain. At his personal invitation, I preached the sermon for his installation at Riverside.

Yeah, Bill's a good name. Who else? Howard replied.

Howard Moody is a possible. Then there's Paul Moore.

These really were good names. Howard Moody was (is) a maverick American Baptist pastor in Greenwich Village who has a long history of championing unpopular but good causes. Bishop Paul Moore was (is) a leading light in the Episcopal Church in New York City and the nation on humanitarian issues.

Bill, I said, trying to prepare him for the worse — a zero response — *I don't know whether I'll be able to reach these guys.*

Somewhat reassuringly, he told me *All you can do is try.*

I spent the rest of the evening putting the finishing touches on my Christmas Sunday sermon. The Damascus proposition had to go on the back burner for the next twelve hours, at least.

The Christmas services at Canaan in central Harlem went well. I shared with my congregation the prospect that I would be traveling to Syria with a group of religious leaders to seek the release of the only known American prisoner of war, Naval Lieutenant Robert O. Goodman. I asked for their prayers to accompany us on this mission of mercy. This was the first time in my sixteen year tenure that pastor and people would not be together as one year dies and another is born. After service as hundreds of members tendered their personal best wishes, I could feel the anticipation building up in me as I prepared for this journey to Damascus.

Mrs. Walker and I shared a quiet Christmas Day dinner with our only child remaining at home, Earl Maurice. After a half-hearted attempt to watch the Sunday menu of professonal football, I knew I had to get to the task of trying to recruit one or two white preachers. Somewhere between six and seven, I secured the home phone number of Bishop Paul Moore through my good friend and best contact on Episcopal affairs, Frederick Boyd Williams, Pastor of The Church of the Intercession in Harlem. I put it to him straight as to what we were about. He assured me that Paul Moore would go if there was any way he could swing it within his prodigious commitments.

In a few moments I put the call through to Moore and talked with one of his children. Bishop Moore and his wife were out but I was assured he would return my call. It wasn't hard to get Howard Moody's number since we work actively together in the American Baptist Churches of Metropolitan New York. Mrs. Moody answered and told me that Howard was out for the evening but due to the urgency of the call, she would try to get word to him. In each instance, I apologized profusely for this invasion of the family's Christmas holiday season. I underscored the need for rapid response. I mused to myself, *Well, that's it for now; I'll just have to sweat it out and see what happens.*

It wasn't very long before Paul Moore returned my call and I quickly gave him a thumbnail digest of what was proposed in our effort to seek Goodman's release. His response was precisely as Fred had predicted. He liked the idea and was inclined to join us except that he was already committed to go to Nicaragua within two weeks.

Wyatt, I'd love to go but I can't this week. Give Jesse my best. You know we've had him here at St. John's . . . you have our earnest prayers for success.

After a bit of small talk, the conversation ended. If Bishop Paul Moore was in this delegation, it would help mute the criticism that was sure to come for this 'hare-brained scheme' *C'est la vie.*

While I was thinking about how close we had come to getting Paul Moore, Mrs. Moody called and told me that Howard couldn't join us but he wanted to call me personally and explain why. For some reason, I became very defensive and politely said to her that there was no need for him to 'explain.' I knew and trusted Howard Moody's impulses and if he felt he couldn't go, that was good enough for me. If he felt like calling, I'd be glad to speak to him, anytime.

Tell him, to be sure and pray for us, I interjected as the conversation ended. It has struck me as rather curious that I haven't heard from Howard Moody since.

It looked as if our delegation was going to be all Black. I rang Bill Howard in Princeton to see if he had

had any luck with Bill Coffin. Since they had traveled to Iran together during the hostage crisis, Howard had volunteered to contact Riverside's pastor.

Coffin's not available to go Howard began, *but that's not the biggest problem! The volunteers for this mission are all dropping out.*

What's the problem? I asked.

Everyone I've talked to says it's a bad time; I think a couple of them didn't have the money.

My rejoinder was direct. *It's always a bad time to do something when risk and sacrifice are involved. Who's confirmed?* I asked.

Are you still committed? Howard asked hesitantly.

Is an elephant heavy? Of course. I responded.

Well, we have two, you and me, and I'm beginning to have second thoughts.

For a moment I was stunned. I couldn't believe this.

What about Jesse? I queried him.

I talked to him within the hour and he hasn't made a determination whether he should go or not. The campaign thing has him a little worried countered Howard.

What about all those guys in Memphis who said they wanted to go I pressed. It looked like this venture and opportunity was slipping away on inconvenience.

They all said the change in date created the problem. Christmas and New Year's is just too special, I suppose. Howard sounded resigned.

How did the date get changed? I pressed.

The Candidate changed it.

I exploded. *Jesse changes the date for his convenience and we don't know for sure whether he's going or not. That's a fine kettle of fish.*

Howard made no response and neither or us spoke for a few moments. Then, finally, I asked *What about the State Department briefing tomorrow?*

I was unprepared for Howard's response. *That's the other item I wanted to talk about. It has been changed to Tuesday, noon. There's no way I can go to D.C. Tuesday and I want to be sure you are there.*

O.K. I responded with some resignation. *If you can't, you can't.* I was dismayed that the Chairman of our delegation couldn't make the briefing.

Wyatt, since you are going to be there, one or two hard questions need to be raised. Can you stay over for a meeting with Jouejati? Rafic Jouejati is the Syrian Ambassador to the U.S. and Howard informed me this meeting would be at the Howard Inn immediately following the State Department briefing.

I readily consented to this second assignment because in light of all the developments to date, I had some questions that I felt needed straight answers. Only Assad's people would have them or could get them.

No problem. I want to find out from the Ambassador what the program will be when we land in Damascus. I don't want to fly 7000 miles and get off the plane without an agenda.

Howard broke in, *You're right and there at least three considerations I want you to put to Jouejati and I know since you're not bashful, you'll see that these issues are raised.* Howard continued, *Number one, we want a firm committment that we can meet with our counterparts, the religious leaders of Syria; number two, we want to see Goodman; and number three, we must insist on meeting with someone high in the government.*

Howard reasoned that if Jesse Jackson did not accompany us, there was little chance that Assad would meet with us but we should not be shunted to some third level officer of the government.

Howard and I were in total agreement on this matter and I was comfortable with the specifics he had outlined. We said goodnight with the promise to touch base with each other just as soon as I returned from Washington. Despite all of the uncertainties, it looked as if Tuesday's schedule would be the first step on our ROAD TO DAMASCUS.

The Road To Damascus

Tuesday morning after Christmas, the twenty-seventh, was a crisp clear December day. Monday had passed uneventfully except for a call from Bill Howard, double-checking to see if indeed I was going to Washington for the briefing. I caught the 10:00 a.m. shuttle from LaGuardia and arrived at the Howard Inn at 11:20. Jesse Jackson had made this hotel, owned and operated by Howard University, his Washington residence. Several members of his top staff lived here. It had become over the last month, his informal "headquarters."

Sylvia Branch, Jackson's personal secretary and custodian of his arduous travel schedule, ushered me into the Candidate's modest suite. A "pre-briefing" was in process and Jackson was leading the discussion with Dr. Ronald Walters, his foreign policy specialist at his side. I was struck by what seemed to me, an inordinate number of people, perhaps twenty in all.

"The State Department will never be the same after this." I thought to myself. John Bustamante, a Cleveland lawyer and banker; Walter Fauntroy, the Minister-Congressman; Tom Porter, top Policy Adviser to Jackson; the national campaign director, Arnold Pinckney; Florence Tate, Press Secretary; four or five other clergymen, staff and hangers-on. I wondered to myself "Are all these people going to Syria?" It was such a disparate group that I felt the seriousness of the mission had been lost over the week-end. My fears were groundless. Only four of this group made the trip to Damascus; Tom Porter, the press secretary, Eugene Wheeler and this writer.

A few minutes before noon, a caravan of cars left the Howard Inn, police escort-led with sirens wailing.

It was a prelude to what we would experience in Damascus. The Treasury Department had assigned a full Secret Service detail (three shifts) now that Jackson was an announced candidate for the presidency. In this instance, I was impressed with their confidence and professionalism. A little too brusque for me, though. Within minutes, in spite of the capital's mid-day traffic, we arrived at Foggy Bottom, as the State Department is disaffectionately known. A claque of media representatives were on hand behind velvet ropes, shouting questions at Jackson as we swept past them into the main lobby of State. They were temporarily pacified by Jackson's press lady who promised them the Candidate would make a full statement after the briefing.

Special elevators whisked us to the third floor office of Richard Murphy, Assistant Secretary of State and head of the Mid-East section of the U.S. State Department. Without any delay, we were ushered into Mr. Murphy's spacious private office. He was flanked by Bruce Earman and Lawrence Eagleburger, Reagan's Foreign Policy Adviser. I learned much later that Jackson reasoned that the briefing was an indication that the Reagan Administration would not stop us from going to Syria. (He was not anxious to go if Reagan prohibited our going) nor did the briefing mean that State would necessarily be helpful. As it turned out, they were extremely helpful at several points.

After the briefest of introductions and pleasantries, we went immediately to work. Dick Murphy had one of his aides hold up a large map of the locale of our visit and pointed out the geographical relationship of Damascus to Beirut and the Chouf mountains where Goodman's plane was shot down. It struck me imme-

SYRIA
AREA 71,498 sq. mi.
POPULATION 7,585,000
CAPITAL Damascus
LARGEST CITY Damascus
HIGHEST POINT Hermon 9,232 ft.
MONETARY UNIT Syrian pcund
MAJOR LANGUAGES Arabic, French,
Kurdish, Armenian
MAJOR RELIGIONS Islam, Christianity

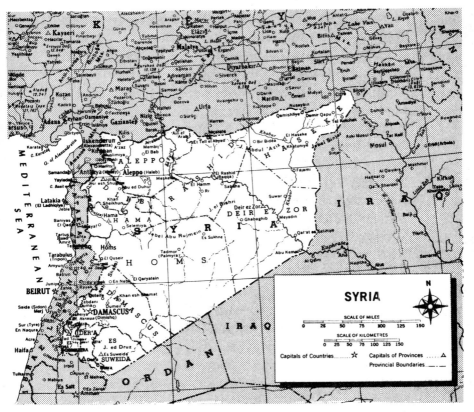

Figure 1

diately that we were going into a war zone. Downtown Damascus was well within range of the Israeli gunboats in the Mediterranean. Beirut was less than fifty miles away. Eagleburger shared with us as much as he could or would about the details of Goodman's capture and where he might be. Murphy made it clear that Robert Paganelli, the U.S. ambassador was the nation's "point man" and all must support him. The State Department's view was that Goodman cannot be used as a bargaining chip. Under no circumstances can Mr. Jackson negotiate for the United States. We were informed that the International Red Cross had made an attempt (without publicity) to secure Goodman's release to no avail.

There were not many questions or answers. At what seemed to be a juncture of awkward silence, Jackson precipitously suggested to Murphy that a smaller meeting might now be more helpful. Murphy readily agreed and Jackson left with Fauntroy and Porter. Eagleburger and Murphy followed to a private office not far away. The rest of us made small talk until they returned some twenty minutes later. It was during this interlude of coffee and tea that I learned that no one present in that group had any intentions of going to Syria at all. I was talking to myself again, *What the hell is going on?*

When the Country Preacher returned, he announced it was time to go. He would make a brief prepared statement to the press with a minimum of questions.* The Howard Inn would be our next stop for an "important meeting with the Syrian ambassador."

The news briefing was short and hectic. Jackson outlined carefully the parameters of our mission. We would be seeking Goodman's release on "humani-

*See Appendix "A."

20

News briefing at State Department. Shown with Jackson are Congressman Walter Fauntroy (r) and Florence Tate (l).

tarian grounds." It was evident to me already that the media was licking its chops, waiting for Jesse Jackson to fall on his face. The tenor of the questioning all had the ring that Jackson was in over his head on this one. I must say, the candidate's aplomb was such that he appeared never to be touched or affected by the snide character of some of the questions.

I'm sorry, but we must go now. Thank you for coming Jackson said, almost abruptly. He nor the media knew at this moment, that they were inextricably bound together in the top news story of the year.

Upon our return to the Howard Inn, the entire group converged on Jackson's suite. Rafic Jouejati was in an adjoining room. The candidate selected about nine or ten of us to join him and Jouejati next door. As we entered, Jouejati rose enthusiastically to greet us, one by one. Jackson took care of the individual introductions and the meeting commenced.

You all know why we are here and I want to express my appreciation to the Ambassador for joining us. I know we should have come to you. Jackson began. *Perhaps you would like to begin Brother Jouejati.*

Rafic Jouejati, at first glance, might be taken for a "heavy" in a Hollywood mystery picture. Deepset, piercing eyes that met at a pronounced aquiline nose. Unsmiling, his countenance seemed brooding. It was the receding hairline, I think, that made me think of Sydney Greenstreet. The moment he began to speak, the warmth and intensity of his personality came through.

I want you to know I am a Christian Arab, he began. *This thing that you propose can have very great consequences . . .* The gist of his straightforward and passionate statement was that the U.S. had many friends in Syria and this effort might well augur for better relations between the two nations. He was very candid. If this could be done (freeing Goodman), Jesse Jackson was the man who could do it.

When he finished speaking, I moved to the attack without any hesitation. If possible, I wanted to catch the four o'clock shuttle to New York.

Mr. Ambassador, several of us have some concern about traveling this distance without some specific assurances about what will take place in Damascus. It felt like he was looking through me with those eyes. A thin smile creased his face. I continued, *The assurances of which I speak are three in number.*

I outlined the three concerns agreed upon with Howard; meeting with our religious counterparts, a visit with Goodman and an audience with some "high" government official.

I interjected at the mention of the third item that we would like to meet with President Assad, but since none of us were heads of state, we understand that that would violate international protocol. However (he was smiling broadly now), we would like to meet with someone in the higher echelons of the Syrian government.

No complications. was his immediate response.

"What, no coded cables to his superiors in Damascus?" I thought, talking to myself again. This was too easy.

Without reservations, Mr. Ambassador, you guarantee that all three assurances can be met! I asked for emphasis.

Absolutely, no question! Jouejati replied.

My main work for that day was completed and shortly thereafter I excused myself and caught the four o'clock shuttle to New York. As the plane circled to land at LaGuardia in the winter darkness, I felt armed with what we needed for a meaningful mission to seek the release of this Black flier. Ready or not Damascus, here we come.

From all that I had gathered from my several hours visit in Washington, D.C., our scheduled departure was still set for Wednesday, the 28th, tomorrow. Once settled at home, I rang up Bill Howard in Princeton and gave him a full report on the day's events. He was more than pleased but began to waffle on the question of his firm commitment to go I had sensed in Jesse Jackson, earlier that day, the impulse to join us in our journey to Damascus, though he had been careful not to commit himself to the media.

What about Jesse's going! This was a trial balloon to find out if Howard knew something I didn't know.

He hasn't made his decision yet, Howard replied. *I think he's trying to get some reaction from Reagan.*

I pressed Howard as to who was firmly committed. His answer disarmed me.

Louis Farrakhan and Wyatt Tee Walker.

Only two of us! What about you! I shot back.

Personally, he began, *I think we need some indication from the Syrians as to whether they're in fact going to release him or not.*

Preacher I howled in mock disbelief, *where is your faith!*

I'm sure I said more than was necessary about this being a faith-journey and to know the outcome before we left, somehow did violence to the whole spiritual rationale for our going in the first place. After my long diatribe, I felt I had convinced Howard of the moral imperative of our mission in spite of its outcome, one way or the other. Two days later, after we were airborne, Howard confessed to me that this heated conversation had helped to resolve some of his doubts about the wisdom of going to Damascus.

Wednesday morning was one of those gray, overcast days of winter with a prediction of rain. There was a funeral scheduled for 10:00 a.m. at my church in Harlem. Dorothy Wright, a solid member from a large family in Canaan, had been killed in an auto accident a block from her home in the Bronx. Just before the services began, Bill Howard called from his office at 475 Riverside Drive, the so-called "God-Box in Manhattan.*" He informed me that the departure set for 7:00 p.m. the same evening had been postponed for at least a day. I had to cut him off with the explanation that I could not keep this grief-stricken family waiting.

O.K., but can you talk on a conference call with me and Jesse and perhaps the Syrian ambassador in an hour!

*The Interchurch Center houses more than 40 denominational offices.

24

I'll be waiting. I assured him.

At 11:10 the conference call came through. Jackson, in command as always, stated the reasons for the postponement but sounded prepared to go. I seized the initiative and gave a digest of the same sermon I had laid on Howard the evening before about the moral imperatives that demanded our going to Syria. I had almost forgotten that Jouejati was on the line also and he quickly offered his encouragement. When questioned by Howard about his candid assessment of our chances, the Syrian ambassador made it very clear, that whatever our chances for success, they would be materially better if Jesse Jackson were in the group. Jackson's enormous respect in the Mid-East, in his judgment, was a tremendous plus.

When the conference call ended some forty minutes later, the die had been cast, despite the thin ranks of our mission. Two days ago, it seemed like everyone and his brother was going; now we were struggling to put together enough people for a quartet. Well, the Lord will provide, I thought.

With the postponement, the rest of the day seemed to drag by. My personal physician, Aaron Wells, had gotten wind of my proposed Mid-East odyssey and insisted that I come by for a check-up before leaving. Like many Black men, I am afflicted with episodes of hypertension, the silent killer. To my utter chagrin, my pressure was abnormally high.

You can't go like this, Reverend, he told me bluntly.

I explained the immense importance of the mission (all of which he already understood) but he wouldn't budge. Unless I would go home immediately to rest and get my pressure down, he would not allow me to go under any circumstances. He would permit me to make preparation to go with the provision that on the way to Kennedy, I must swing by his office for another examination.

As fate would have it, on the way to my home in Yonkers, as I entered the Saw Mill River Parkway from the Deegan Expressway, my Mercury Marquis skidded in the light rain that had begun to fall around two o'clock. In my frantic effort to come out of the skid, I struck the curbing on the left side and blew a tire. The rain turned to snow and for the next three hours I was engaged in the cold, damp task of changing a tire with those new-fangled lug keys that protect? your hub caps from thieves. What a miserable afternoon! I needed that extra stress like I needed a hole in my head.

Finally I was rescued by our middle son, Robert. Right on his heels was a CBS television crew who wanted an interview about the postponed departure. Yes, the trip was definitely on (I fudged). I was certain that Mr. Jackson would go and the consequences to his Presidential campaign were not nearly as important as what we were about as it related to Goodman and setting a new climate in the Mid-East.

Once home, warmed and fed, I called Jesse at the Howard Inn in D.C. He was on another phone so I asked for Euguene Wheeler, his travel secretary. I knew from past experience Wheeler would get a message to the candidate. I impressed upon Wheeler to make Reverend Jackson know, that all things considered, we needed to go to Syria even if it were only he, Farrakhan and myself. Within a half hour of this brief exchange, I was in another world — asleep!

The next morning, Thursday, the twenty-ninth, I slept late. I reasoned that if this indeed turned out to be departure day, I should be well-rested for the long flight to Damascus via Frankfurt. My wife and I went to a local shopping mall where I picked up ten rolls of slide film just in case there was an opportunity for picture taking. By the time we returned to the house, my personal secretary, Lorraine Springsteen had called to tell me that Jackson's office had called. The instructions were terse and direct; the delegation was to meet at TWA's International terminal at 4 p.m. for a press briefing and leave for Frankfurt at 6:55. Be sure to bring passport and fare. I called Dr. Wells immediately and informed him the mission was on. He only rejoinder was to stop by his office on the way to the airport for a final check on my blood pressure.

My bag was packed in thirty minutes. Our return was scheduled for Tuesday; that meant four days in Damascus. Four shirts and one dark suit and the blazer and slacks I travel in would do the trick.

My blood pressure was fine and we arrived at TWA about 4:45. Our middle son, Robert, and my pastoral assistant, Reverend Knight had eagerly volunteered to accompany me to Kennedy. At this point in time, both of them had a keener sense of the historic moment than I. Inside the terminal, my name was on the paging system but the instruction was unclear. With a little checking, I learned Mr. Jackson's party was meeting in the Ambassador's lounge in the domestic terminal. At the mezzanine level, we saw the TV lights about thirty yards away.

This is it! I chortled with satisfaction.

The media was assembled in full force. I scanned their ranks, saw all three networks plus Channel 5, 9 and 11. We tried to force our way through TWA's security personnel. Their agent was a rather generously proportioned Black lady who took my jocularity too seriously. She made me understand quickly that she wasn't giving anybody a hard time, she was doing her job. Then at the lounge entrance was the Secret Service detail. I caught the eye of one of several agents I recognized from Memphis. Just as we gained entrance, Jesse Jackson was leaving.

Come on Wyatt, I need you at the press briefing.

I dropped my bags and did a 180 degree turn and followed the Country Preacher to the press area. It was during the next few hectic moments that I learned the composition of the ecumenical delegation. In addition to Jackson, Farrakhan and myself, I was gratified to see Bill Howard join the circle in front of the klieg lights. Dr. Thelma Adair (we always overlook women), a Presbyterian, Ed Theobald, a Roman Catholic layman, the Rev. Jack Mendelsohn, a Unitarian with us two Baptist and a Muslim, rounded out the group.

Jesse Jackson is an earnest family man. His wife Jacqueline was enroute to Nicaragua with a women's peace group, so he elected to bring along two of his sons, Jesse Jr. and Jonathan. There was of course, the support staff, Dr. Thomas Porter, senior policy adviser, Dr. Andrew Thomas, Jackson's personal physician, Ms. Florence Tate, press secretary, Minister Farrakhan's personal aide, Minister Akbar Muhammed and Ms. Julia Jones, the campaign's official photographer, a volunteer. Ms. Jones came from D.C. to record the candidate's departure but flew with us to Syria *sans* passport or luggage.* One full Secret Service section was already in Damascus and two full sections would accompany us from the States.

At the close of the press briefing, we retraced our steps to the Ambassador's Lounge. There, I learned from Florence Tate, that in addition to the networks,

*Alphabetical list appears in Appendix "B."

the *New York Times*, the *Washington Post*, *Time Magazine* and the wire services were all sending correspondents. *Newsweek*'s Liz Holton, who had broken the story about Rumsfeld's silence, was already in Damascus. Two of the networks correspondents were Afro-Americans as were the reporters from the *New York Times* and *Time Magazine*. A young photo-journalist from *Johnson Publications*, D. Michael Cheers, was the only representative from Black media.

After a brief round of introductions to Goodman's mother and some goodnatured posing for picture-taking, we were on our way to board Flight 476 to Frankfurt.

The flight to Frankfurt was uneventful so far as the mission to Syria was concerned. By chance, I was seated next to Louis Farrakhan, whom I had known for some twenty years. Despite the fact that we had worked "different sides of the street" in the liberation struggle of Black people, each of us had always accorded to the other a great amount of respect and affection. During this long plane ride, I realized that I only knew him professionally. This journey to Damascus tightened the personal bond between us. He took such great delight in the portable typewriter that I use for composition when I'm traveling. It's a Brother (of all things) EP-22 that weighs less than four pounds. Its great asset is that it is noiseless, has a two page memory bank, a 16 character correcton facility and operates on a computer mode. Its slight size makes it possible to slip it into a briefcase. Never has a transatlantic crossing passed so swiftly.

We landed in Frankfurt in murky weather. The mission members and staff along with Mr. Jackson were escorted under heavy security to a rather remote

VIP room. Our Secret Service detail was supplemented by West German police. Jackson barked a command to Wheeler and Porter to get everyone together. As we sat or stood, the candidate with obvious weariness from the flight and the previous two days, simply reminded all of us of the seriousness of our purpose and announced:

I want Wyatt to serve as Chief of Portocol for this mission and Tom Porter and Dr. Thomas will provide whatever back-up is required. Having said that, he turned on his heel and concluded, *I've got to get some sleep!* In retrospect, I was never more ready for this particular task.

Over the last twenty years, international travel had been "my thing." Syria would be the seventy-first country I had visited. This was my 19th trip to the Middle East; six times to Egypt, four times to Jordan, twice to Lebanon, eighteen times to Israel and the Occupied Territories of the West Bank. For Martin Luther King's Nobel Peace Prize ceremony, I served as press attache and during the Rockefeller years made state visits to West Africa, South America and the Soviet Union. My involvement with the World Peace Movement had carried me all over Eastern Europe. I was ready.

Dwight Ellison, a section leader of the Secret Service detail, who happened to be Black with roots in Throop County, Georgia, informed me that Mr. Jackson instructed him to brief me and whomever else I chose on what to expect in Damascus in terms of the security concerns. The briefing was thorough and detailed. I remember having the distinct impression that this was going to be far more dangerous for Jesse Jackson than I had anticipated. I was brought up short by Ellison's last admonition: *At no time do we want*

Reverend Jackson to be a standing target!

Only once before in my life had I ever had the impulse to decide that if I knew a bullet was coming, I would be willing to take it instead of its intended victim; that was years ago for Martin Luther King, Jr. I took that vow a second time in Frankfurt, Germany for Jesse Louis Jackson. The revelation of the presence of so many disparate political and religious communities in Damascus, especially the Khomeini group, prompted this decision in me. We had to be prepared for any and every thing.

At the end of the briefing, to which the entire group gave rapt attention (I saw no need to exclude anyone), I noticed whatever light-heartedness had been present, completely disappeared. The soberness of the moment visibly affected Jonathan and Jesse Jr. They both realized that they might be witnesses to their father's serious injury or death.

I plunged into my new assignment immediately while the other members of the mission scattered to sleep or visit the duty free shops in the main terminal. I drafted first a DAILY MEMO form that I knew would be useful for the accurate transmission of information. In the compressed time of our visit, I assumed correctly that the time pressures would be great and rounding up fourteen people quickly could be sticky. While the memo form was being duplicated through the courtesy of an American embassy official whom I have yet to identify, I developed a code of General Decorum for our stay in Syria.* Later when I distributed these to every mission member and staff, I made car assignments and indicated on the General Decorum memo, "Car assignments are permanent and under no circumstances to be changed." This

*See Appendix "C."

mandate later proved to be invaluable with the sudden movements of our group in Damascus.

By the time I gained Mr. Jackson's approval of all that I had done relative to the briefing and the proposed memos, it was time to enplane for Damascus. Our flight was airborne at 2:00 p.m. for the three and a half hour flight to Syria's capital city. At 7:05, our Lufthansa flight touched down on the tarmac of the Damascus aerodrome. A few minutes earlier, Ellison fully informed of my role as Chief of Protocol, let me know that the Syrians had decided on the deplaning procedures and as far as he was concerned, that plan would be followed to the letter. The Secret Service would take Mr. Jackson off first after the commercial passengers had deplaned. The rest of the mission and the press corps would exit via the rear door of the plane.

Roger and Ten-four, I said playfully.

Some of the press corps took some mild exception to the plan, complaining that they needed to have pictures of Mr. Jackson arriving in Syria. I was as firm with them as Ellison had been with me and all of us followed the procedure as outlined by the Syrian government. HELLO DAMASCUS!*

*See Appendix "D" and "E".

Three Assurances Fulfilled

My only recollection of the Damascus air terminal is a crowded "VIP" room including the American embassy officials and the designees of the Assad government. I would remember later that one of them was a Deputy Foreign Secretary Issam Annayel. Of course the U.S. Ambassador, Robert Paganelli, was on hand to welcome this delegation of American visitors. He did not seem like a happy man. With him was a staff aide, Bruce Streathorn, who proved to be extremely helpful and considerate during our entire stay in Damascus. Someone inquired of Mr. Jackson as to the identity of his protocol officer.

Wyatt. he barked. *This gentleman is in charge of protocol for the government of Syria. The two of you need to get together.* A smallish man in a gray suit extended his card to me and we shook hands warmly. In my best Arabic, I greeted him.

A Salaam aleikem! Kif Halak.

With ever so slight a twinkle in his eye, he returned the greeting, *Aleikem a salaam. Al Hamdu L'Ullah.*

The card bore the name Khalil Abu Hadad in raised script. The card I handed him for his reference was my Freedom National Bank card which bore my name as Chairman of the Board. The din and press of the crowded room was overwhelming and he quickly led me through a door at the far end of the room. It was a hallway which became our antechamber that would set in motion one of the most spectacular occurrences in American foreign policy.

Hadad outlined for me hurriedly the agenda for the next day's schedule (Saturday). A meeting with the foreign minister at 10:00 a.m., perhaps a visit with

DAILY MEMO

DATE 12/31 DAY SATURDAY

TODAY'S SCHEDULE

9:00 A.M. MTG. WITH REV. JACKSON #367

10-12 FOREIGN MINISTRY

LUNCH & PRESS BRIEFING

2-5 PRESIDENT ASSAD & GOODMAN ?

DEPARTURE TIME FROM HOTEL **9:45 A.M.**
2:00 P.M.?

RETURN TO HOTEL **12:00 N**
5:00 P.M.

Car Assignments Are Permanent for Duration of Mission

NO EXCEPTIONS

TOMORROW THIS AFTERNOON TONITE —

RELIGIOUS LEADERS (NOT SET)

RECEPTION U.S. ←
EMBASSY

Figure 2

Khalil Abu Hadad.

President Assad and Goodman in the afternoon and an evening meeting with the religious leaders of Syria.

Is there anything tonight? I asked.

No. Hadad responded. *As soon as we are finished here, we shall go immediately to your hotel and I will see you at 8:30 tomorrow morning.*

As we stepped back into the room, Mr. Jackson was finishing up the introductions of the entire party to the Syrians, Paganelli and staff. He announced that he would make a brief arrival statement for the benefit of the news media, all of whom had been excluded from this gathering.

Before we do that, however, I'd like us to have a prayer of thanks for our safe journey. Minister Farrakhan, would you lead us in prayer?

In flawless Arabic, Farrakhan began to give thanks to God with a traditional prayer from the Holy Qua'ran. I opened my eyes to observe the reaction of our hosts and every Syrian had his eyes open and exchanging faint smiles while this Black brother from Chicago, was praying in their language!

In a few minutes, the Rev. Jesse Louis Jackson flanked by his motley fellow travelers, stood before a broad array of the world's media. The weariness and burden of this new challenge, was beginning to show ever so slightly. The onslaught of huskiness in his voice was a dead giveaway.

Arrival at Damascus Aerodrome. (l-r) Jackson, Issam Annayeh, Robert Paganelli and M. William Howard (far right).

It seemed that the whirlwind was upon us. Some mild indecision as to whether we would ride in embassy cars or those provided by the Syrians. It was quickly resolved with my gentle reminder of the permanent car assignments.

Just stay with your partners and take a good look at your driver! I announced.

I had carefully grouped our delegation by car assignments following Mr. Jackson's arrival statement. The pattern of our transportation in Damascus was set in concrete with our exit from the airport. In Frankfurt, Ellison had alerted me that only two persons would be allowed to ride in Mr. Jackson's car. I assigned Bill Howard and Thelma Adair. A full car of Secret Service men was in front and behind the Jackson vehicle. In front and behind each of these cars was a complement of Syrian secret police; then a motorcycle escort at each end, preceded and followed by a small weapons carrier vehicle. Somewhere in this line of cars was a "back-up" car with Secret Service men. At the rear of this line followed all the other cars of the delegation. I'm sure we were some sight to behold as we careened through the streets of one of the oldest cities in the world.

With sirens wailing, we sped to the Sheraton-Damascus. Upon our arrival, we were directed to our pre-registered rooms, all on the third floor of this downtown hotel. Mr. Jackson was ensconced in 367, a two bedroom suite he shared with Wheeler.

As I emerged from my room down the hall from "the Leader" as I began to refer to Jackson, Bill Howard told me that Jesse would like to see everyone in his suite at nine. It was about eight-thirty then.

Before we eat? I asked rhetorically.

He said at nine. Howard answered.

O.K. I'll round them up.

Everyone was present at nine. Jackson briefly reviewed the purpose of our mission and admonished us to pray especially for the Holy Spirit to guide him during the discussions the next day.

Goodman's fate depends on our spiritual preparedness. I need your prayers.

This was as solemn a moment as I can recall during the entire Damascus adventure. We joined hands and Bill Howard led us in prayer. We quietly went our separate ways in twos or threes to eat, browse or retire.

Later that evening, after dinner with Dr. Thomas and Tom Porter, I framed out the first memo for Saturday's schedule, December 31st.* Our third floor location was adjacent to the command centers of the Secret Service (opposite Jackson's room), the Syrian secret police and the American embassy. Streathorn had walked me through their post near the elevators. It had everything we needed. Electric typewriters, desks, telephones, a big Xerox machine, stationery supplies, etc. Once I cleared the memo with Jesse, my next stop was this embassy command post, available and staffed around the clock. I was in business!

I took the room list and slipped a memo under the door of every member of our party. I routinely advised the Secret Service at their command post of every schedule and the prospect of change. Long before midnight, all the bases had been touched. I showered and went to bed.

I slept fitfully until the alarm on my travel clock awakened me. To save time, I ordered breakfast through room service. By the time it arrived I was dressed. I have always followed the adage, ''Eat a good breakfast!'' Some few minutes after seven-thirty, I was in Jackson's suite for any early morning instructions. He was wide awake but not yet dressed. He was reading some policy statements prepared by Tom Porter. Some unfinished tea and toast was beside the bed.

Wyatt, this memo idea is good. Ask everyone to meet here at nine.

O.K. Leader I replied.

I quickly made the rounds of the rooms, knocking and yelling. *First call!* Tom Porter and Florence Tate were already dressed. Hadad was due at 8:30 so I

*See Figure 2.

38

started to the lobby. Enroute, I met Dwight Ellison of the Secret Service who asked if I could manage to have the entire party in their cars before Reverend Jackson would come down. Security considerations, he said. "No problem," I assured him.

Hadad was in the hotel lobby having Arabic coffee with a colleague from the Foreign Ministry. He was introduced to me as Hamzeh Hamzeh and we exchanged business cards. He was about the same height as Hadad, but dark-haried and rather hooded eyes of an Oriental.

"Dr. Walker" he read from the card with a quizzical smile. I did not know then how important a role this little man was going to play in the drama of Goodman's release.

Hamzeh Hamzeh

Hadad indicated everything was in order. I showed him the memo I had circulated and he quickly noted that there was no word yet on the meeting with Assad. We exchanged a few pleasantries and I returned to Jackson's suite for the nine o'clock meeting.

Upon entering the suite, I was a little surprised that everyone was in place. Jackson was sipping a cup of tea. He looked diplomatically elegant in a smartly cut, dark blue suit, soft blue shirt and foulard tie held at a jaunty angle with the gold collar pins currently in vogue. There was very little talking by Jackson, just the brief reminder as to what we were about and then we joined hands for prayer. Our lady mission member, Thelma Adair was asked to pray. A Baptist preacher's daughter, Presbyterian pastor's widow, first Black woman moderator of the Presbyterian Church in the U.S., currently head of Church Women United; this Queens College professor of education with a Ph.D., was in her element. More than once I thanked the Lord for her presence.

After the prayer, I asked everyone to vacate the suite and go to the lobby and load up according to car assignments. Jonathan and Jesse Jr. resisted, expressing their desire to come down with their father.

Now fellas, I began, *your Daddy put me in charge of this operation and this is the way we're going to do it. Let's move it!* I was a little harsh with them but there wasn't time to explain then.

Hadad let me know in our earlier meeting that the Foreign Ministry was just minutes away and with the police escort it would not be necessary to leave the hotel until 9:55. On this first day, amid the anxieties surrounding the trip, the ten minutes sitting in the assigned cars seemed interminable. Jesse Jr. jumped out with the protest that he had left something in his room.

Jesse I commanded, *get back in that car!* I was not going to let anyone break the discipline of the mission. He quickly complied.

At 9:54, I gave the Secret Service detail the cue that

everyone was in their assigned cars and Mr. Jackson should be brought down. The Secret Service procedure at my signal was to send two agents on an elevator with no passengers to the third floor where another two or more would be waiting. Once the elevator was on the third floor, still other agents in Mr. Jackson's suite would then exit the room with Mr. Jackson. They were absolutely serious about Jackson never being a standing target.

On this first morning and subsequent days, Jesse Louis Jackson would be seated in his car with Bill and Thelma in less than a minute. Whatever one's disposition toward the Secret Service, you have to admit that they know what they're doing.

Dr. Thomas, Jackson's physician, Tom Porter and I were always in the last car. Thomas had a bad knee and could not move with much agility and Tom Porter and I needed to be in constant touch. Off we sped to the Foreign Ministry to meet with Abdel Khaddam, Foreign Secretary of the Republic of Syria.

Foreign Ministry building, Syrian Arab Republic.

In spite of being a part of the official entourage, when we alighted from our car at the nondescript head-quarters of the Foreign Ministry, the narrow street in front of the Foreign Ministry could not accommodate the ten or twelve cars of our retinue. Consequently, Thomas and I were nearly a city block away from the entrance. Jesse Jackson was already inside in a third floor conference room. I sent Tom Porter on ahead because I knew Jackson would be looking for him immediately. The first person I saw, once inside, was Hamzeh Hamzeh. I asked if there were an elevator available for Dr. Thomas.

Of course. he replied unsmiling.

He accompanied us to the spacious conference room on the third floor. Jackson was making the introductions and I was relieved to see Hadad present. There was something about this man and his demeanor that drew me to him.

Photo opportunity at initial meeting at Foreign Ministry.

Abdel Khaddam and Jesse Jackson sat directly op-posite each other at a huge ornate conference table. Howard was to Jackson's right and Jack Mendelssohn to his left. Khaddam was flanked on his right by a heavily mustachioed translator who served during our entire stay. To the right and left were several other aides. The rest of our mission and staff took seats around the table, spilling over onto the "Syrian" side.

Jackson was the first to speak in short cryptic phrases both for clarity and the facility of translation. Farrakhan, seated at the far end of the table, was asked to begin this session with prayer. Once again, he intoned a prayer in Arabic from the Holy Qua' ran. I have heard many a speech in my time, but never had I heard so passionate a plea as Jackson made in the case for the release of Goodman. These phrases were soon to be historic — "break the cycle of pain" and "lower the temperature in the Mid-East." At the end of Jackson's appeal, Khaddam responded through the translator in an almost diffident manner.

Abdel Halim Khaddam with interpreter.

You ask us to do what is difficult to do. The reality of the situation was that it would be a devasting blow to the morale of the Syrian troops who were the objects of Goodman's attack. There was no way he could as Foreign Minister recommend the release of the "enemy."

When Khaddam had concluded his response that had no hint of promise, Jackson leaped to the attack. Leaning forward on his elbows, almost nose to nose with Khaddam, the country preacher told Khaddam he appreciated all that he had said but "we do not come seeking justice, we're asking for mercy." The discussion must rise above government to government level. The basis of the appeal is "humanitarian and moral."

No one spoke in our delegation except Jackson. There was some note-passing from Tom Porter and Bill Howard. Khaddam alone spoke for the Syrians. Following the second exchange, Jackson suggested to the Foreign Minister that perhaps the discussions were at a point now, where a smaller group might be more productive. Khaddam agreed readily. Jackson announced to us that he had previously spoken to those who would accompany him to Khaddam's private office. He left with Porter, Mendelsohn and Howard.

Mission members in Khaddam meeting. (l-r) Adair, Jesse, Jr., Howard and Jackson)

During the twenty-five to thirty minute period of their absence, tea and coffee was served. Once again the atmosphere was subdued and I had no "feel" as to

Farrakhan and Walker in Khaddam meeting.

how we were doing. It was just too early to tell. I did learn in conversation with Hadad that his last diplomatic assignment was a five year stint in Lagos, Nigeria. Right or wrong, I surmised that if the Syrians had picked Hadad as chief of protocol for this mission, they had done so with careful design. They wanted someone who understood the dynamics of color.

When Jackson and his special committee returned, Khaddam took his leave of us with the hope that something might be done to satisfy the interests of both parties.

Our return to the Sheraton was as swift as our departure. Florence Tate had promised the news corps a briefing upon our return. Mr. Jackson went directly to his suite while Florence organized the logistics for the briefing scheduled for an ample room off the main lobby of the hotel. Our presence had already created a stir among the guests and Damascenes. Tension and excitement was in the air. When I arrived in Mr. Jackson's suite, the Secret Service detail suggested that for the briefing, all the media should be assembled and the doors closed; then they would bring the Reverend down in the same manner as they had for our earlier departure. This procedure was maintained throughout our stay in Syria. Once Mr. Jackson was in place, no one would be allowed to enter or leave until the briefing was at an end. My high visibility with the Secret Service, frequently made me an exception to this rule.

It is no exaggeration to say that the media's eagerness could be compared to vultures whose prey had come into view. This initial briefing following the discussion with the number two man in Syria's government was bedlam. The questions were fast and furious. Through it all, Jackson gave little indication of what he thought the prospect might be at this early stage. Frequently, he corrected the news media about the use of the word "negotiations."

There are no negotiations becaue we have nothing to give. We are making a moral appeal.

During the break, following the press briefing, I answered a page in the hotel lobby. A Mr. Inaan Raad introduced himself to me as a Chairman of the Lebanese National Democratic Front. He was very anxious to meet with Mr. Jackson. I promised him I'd find out if it were possible. It would not be today; perhaps tomorrow.

In a very short while, Hadid reappeared. I had not seen him since the meeting with Khaddam. The visit with Goodman was "being arranged" but something would have to be done about the media. Security concerns would not allow the entire press complement to accompany us.

I found Florence Tate near the site of the press briefing and brought her up to date on the Goodman visit. She was on the horns of a small dilemma as to how to include a Damascus-based TV crew with the restrictions just imposed. Neither of us wanted anything to block the visit but practically, we needed maximum coverage.

We'd better let the Leader know about this, I concluded.

In Room 367, Jesse Jackson had been meeting with some key individuals, in and out of the Syrian government, who had access to President Assad. He reasoned correctly, that any and everyone around Assad needed to have a clear focus of our mission. He was in deep conversation with Khaled Fahoum, Chairman of the Palestine National Council. I caught his attention and whispered the grave urgency of settling the press thing.

Uncharacteristically, Jackson quickly answered, *You handle it!* Much has been written and said about Jackson's swashbuckIng style and his penchant for making or unmaking decisions without benefit of advisors input. In the Damascus experience, I found this to be an unwarranted criticism.

Florence Tate was waiting in the lobby for instructions. I relayed the message to her with the view that since she was constantly dealing with the media, just give me her recommendation and I'd back it and take any heat connected with her decision.

On the basis of Hadad's instructions surrounding the Goodman visit, around three in the afternoon, Tom Porter and I alerted everyone that we were on stand-by. Florence did a herculean job in this instance, keeping the media at bay and yet close enough to be rounded up at a minute's notice. A part of the great apprehension was that the Syrians had a complete cloak of secrecy as to where Goodman was billeted.

At 3:30, Khalil Hadad informed me it was a "go" with Goodman at four. I touched the bases; Reverend Jackson received the first alert, then the Secret Service and the embassy staff. All mission members were to be in their assigned vehicles at 3:55. Putting two and two together, I knew then that Goodman was not far away.

Following our procedure established earlier that day, as Mr. Jackson came through the lobby, a network journalist broke through the cordon just enough to complain to Mr. Jackson that she had followed his campaign faithfully and was being shut out of the biggest story to date.

Florence Tate and I had agreed on a "pool" arrangement for the Goodman visit. One TV crew of three, a print journalist, one color and one black and white photographer. Of course, Mr. Jackson's official photographer, Julia Jones, was permitted to go along with Michael Cheers of Johnson Publications (we had to look out for the Black press).

Jackson's glance shot immediately to me. *Can you work something out for them Wyatt?*

It's all set Leader. Security! I shot back.

Can't we do something? he asked.

You told me to handle it and it's all arranged with Hadad. I don't want to look like we don't know what we're doing.

The minutes were ticking away and the Secret Service were edgy; they wanted to get Jackson into his car and the Syrians wanted to get on with the visit.

Do you mind if I ask Hadad? he said hesitantly.

That's up to you, I responded curtly.

This was the only instance of any real difference between us and we settled it privately early the next morning. This exchange created the only confusion during our entire stay in Syria. Hadad was firm on the security measures and we left the Sheraton with sirens screaming. The other media people assuming wrongly that now, all may come, commandeered cars and taxis and followed our entourage in hot pursuit. The Syrians were utterly confused and allowed them inside the compound gates where Goodman was being held, two minutes from the Sheraton-Damascus.

When I arrived at the entrance to the building, the media folk were everywhere, almost a mini-riot.

Florence Tate was a little distraught. *What are we going to do, Wyatt?*

Follow the plan, darlin', just like we outlined it. No more, no less. I was glad Jesse Jackson was already inside.

Our mission members were assembled in a large room, probably the commandant's office. I learned subsequent to our visit, we were on the premises of a military compound in Damascus. Ambassador Paganelli was abed with the flu and sent his first deputy, William A. Rugh. During the twenty minute wait for Goodman to be delivered for the visit, it was discovered that Jonathan had been left behind. Jesse Jr. explained that he had knocked on his door and couldn't get an answer *and Rev. Walker said we must not be late!* (smile). Through someone's good offices, Jonathan arrived in time.

This was the second best meeting during our stay in Syria. Goodman, as the nation learned later is a real pro. His confidence, poise and wit was striking and we all loved him immediately. When asked what he wanted most for Christmas, he quickly answered,

A plane ticket!
Cheers called for him to look this way for Jet magazine.

A cover story, I hope. he said kiddingly.

Another reporter asked when did he find out about Rev. Jackson's coming.

Goodman replied that his captor kept saying "Jackson" and he thought, "Reggie?" "Michael?" then he knew it had to be Jesse Jackson.

All of this exchange took place as a part of the repartee of the news people first entrance into the room. When the serious interviews began, Goodman, touchingly said, the first thing he wanted to say was to express his condolences to the family of Mark Lange, his friend and pilot, who was killed when they were shot down in the Chouf Mountains of Lebanon. One irrascible news person asked did Goodman know how many people he had killed. Jackson quickly ruled that the question was totally inappropriate. He was appreciative of the mountain of mail he had

Jackson delivers letter to Goodman.

received and thanked everyone for their prayers and concern.

What do you think of Rev. Jackson's efforts to free you? probed another questioner.

I'm a naval flier, not a politician. I just hope that whoever's in charge of getting me released will do it as soon as possible.

Jackson personally delivered a letter to Goodman from his mother and told him of the great interest in America that he would soon be released.

The press corps was dismissed and we had some "private time" with Goodman. He shared with us what this ordeal had been like since his capture and allowed that all in all, he had been treated well. There was plenty of reading material, mostly westerns and TV fare of the fifties and sixties. We all partcipated in a round of picture taking with him as Reverend Jackson made the personal introductions of all those pre-

Farrakhan, Goodman and Jesse Jackson.

sent including Rugh from the embassy. At this juncture, Jackson asked for a Bible to leave with this naval pilot who didn't have one. The only person with a Bible was Louis Farrakhan, a Muslim! We all had a good laugh over this. After signing our names in this recent gift, we joined hands and Farrakhan and Bill Howard led us in prayer.

That single hour spent with this young Black flier was alone worth all the energy expended in coming to Syria. As we said our good-byes, the reality deepened that we might not see him again for a long time.

A parting prayer.

After a brief stop at the Sheraton, we were on our way again with sirens wailing to meet with the heads of the religious communities in Syria. Earlier in the day, the logistics of our mission, visiting ten or more religious leaders within the parameter of our stay in Syria, was unmanageable. I asked was there some ''neutral'' ground where they might assemble and we would come to them. Hadad arranged for the meeting to be held in the offices of the Ministry of Religion and Endowment.

The second floor offices of the ministry was in central Damascus. Saturday evening traffic was at it's worst and it was New Year's Eve. As I climbed the steps to our destination, it occurred to me that we had not yet been in Damascus twenty-four hours.

The Secretary received us into his chambers promptly at 6 p.m. Damascus time. It was noon on the east coast of the U.S.

As I was soon to learn, this was a pre-meeting and the main meeting was not scheduled for another thirty minutes at the same time when our entire party was expected to attend a reception in our honor at the embassy residence. While Jackson and Howard led the discussion, I found a phone and began to re-adjust our schedule. Bruce Streathearn, the embassy Control Officer, was my best bet. I could not reach him for love nor money. Each time I placed a call, I needed assistance (I never thought I'd miss you Ma Bell). Finally, after twenty minutes of vain attempts, I reached a lady Marine who promised she would transmit the message of our delay to the embassy residence. My guess was that we would arrive about 7:30 p.m., an hour later than scheduled.

My return to the executive offices of the Ministry of Religion and Endowment was at the concluding moments of the dialogue between Jackson and the Syrian government's ombudsman for the broad variety of religious communities, both Christian and Moslem. This was a far cry from the West's Protestant, Catholic and Jew arrangement. Candor requires me to divulge that none of us (with the single exception of Howard) were prepared for the religious diversity we would encounter in the next hour.

Our entire mission was directed into an adjoining conference room where an assembly of Syria's religious leaders had gathered to receive the Reverend Jesse Jackson and Co. Jackson's wise choice of Bill Howard as Chairman of the ecumenical mission was borne out in this meeting which proved later to be crucial. Howard in his previous posts as President of

Meeting with religious leaders.

the National Council of Churches and Commissioner of the Program to Combat Racism of the World Council of Churches, already knew three of these high church figures. The Moslem cadre represented all shades of Islamic thought; Shiite, Alawite (Assad's sect) Sunni and the Christian cadre included the Roman Catholic, Greek Catholic, Syrian Orthodox, Greek Orthodox, the Armenian Orthodox and a single representative for the Protestant community in Syria. Dressed in their distinctive clerical garb, they were quite an impressive sight to behold.*

From time to time, Khalil Abu Hadad would seem to disappear and reappear mysteriously. This occasion was an instance of his "reappearance," I'm sure a part of it was my focus and concentration on details. I motioned for him to join me in a near-by corridor as the introductions began. I should interject here, that in the midst of all that was happening. I was desper-

*See Figure 3.

December 31 Religious Leaders Convocation

KEY TO SEATING

| Sheik Shawkei Ali Gibah College of Islamics | Bishop Abu Mukh Greek Catholic representative of the Patriarch | Sheik Muhammad A. F. Khatbib Teacher, College of Islamics | Sheik Abdullah al Sayyed Teacher, College of Islamics |

Minister Louis Farrakhan

Patriarch Zakka I
Head of the Syrian Orthodox
Church in the World

Rev. M. William Howard

Dr. Ibrahim Salgini
Dean of the College of Islamics
& Jurisdiction

Interpreter

Sheik Ziad Eddin Ayubi
Teacher, College of Islamics

Translator

Rev. Jesse Jackson

**Minister of Religion and
Endowment**

Rev. Jack Mendelsohn

Patriarch Agnatius IV Hazzim
Head of Greek Orthodox
church of the Orient

Dr. Thelma Adair

Dr. Wahdi Zuhaih
Teacher, College of Islamics

Dr. Wyatt Tee Walker

Bishop Samaha
Greek Orthodox Community in
South Syria (Golan Heights)

| The Rev. Adeeb Awad Head of the Protestant Community in Syria (United Presbyterian) | Bishop Kolpakian Armenian Orthodox Church, Syria & Greece | Dr. Muhammad A. L. Earfour Teacher in College of Islamics |

Figure 3

55

**Secretary of Religion & Endowment
and Patriarch Agnatius IV Hazim.**

ately trying to make some personal photographic
record of what was going on.

Khalil, how long do you think this is going to last? I
asked.

Already I felt close enough to call him by his first
name. In his measured elegant English, he responded.

I think about one hour.

An hour! I blurted out. I knew we would never
make the embassy reception as I had promised. *I need
to make a phone call.*

With Hadad's efficient assistance, I quickly
notified the American embassy that there would be a
further delay. Upon my return to the conference
room, the meeting was in full sway. Jackson had
made the introductions and was earnestly pleading
our case for Goodman's release. This proved to be the
toughest meeting of all. In the course of making his
"moral appeal," the Country Preacher in his florid
style mentioned that if Goodman were released, "it
would dry up the tears of his wife and children."
Patriarch Agnatius IV Hazim; with eyes flashing,
countered Jackson's plea by saying,

We are supportive of your efforts to free Lt. Goodman in spite of the fact that we perceive him as an agent of war and death. I ask you, who will wipe away the tears of the villagers on whom the bombs rained death and terror?

Jesse Jackson was as eloquent and creative in his response to the hard line of these religious leaders as he had been with the Foreign Secretary, Abdel Khaddam. I was comfortable when this session ended that hearts had been significantly touched on both sides of the table.

I peeked at my watch and heaved a sigh of relief. It looked as if we would make the Ambassador's residence on the adjusted schedule. I noticed Bill Howard standing around, almost casually. I gently suggested we ought to be making our way to our assigned cars.

Bishop Kolpakian.

Dr. Ibrahim Salgini.

Patriarch Zakka I.

Bishop Samaha.

(l-r) Sheik Shawkei Ali Gibah, Bishop Abu Mukh and Sheik Muhammad A. F. Khatbib

We can't leave yet. They're setting up the conference room for a reception in our honor, he replied.

We can skip that. We've got to get to the embassy residence.

Howard looked me square in the eye. *We can't skip THIS! Let me tell you something Harlem preacher, to leave now without eating with these folk would be the grossest insult. The Ambassador's shin-dig will have to wait. These people have too much influence with Assad. I don't think Paganelli is in position to help us.* I smarted a little under this upbraiding by this mild mannered Christian gentleman but I knew he was excactly right.

Yes Sir, Dr. Howard! I said my myself.

When we arrived at the palatial (by Syrian standards) residence of the American ambassador to Syria, it was 8:40 p.m. Since I was Jackson's protocol officer, it was my responsibility to offer my apologies for our tardiness. In my most courtly Virginia manner, I explained to Mrs. Paganelli the unavoidable circumstances that detained us. A rather attractive dark-haired lady, Mrs. Paganelli was the epitome of graciousness. We met the ambassador's two daughters and a male house guest of Chinese extraction. The full complement of embassy personnel were present; Bruce Strathearn, Marc Carlisle and Thomas "Pat" O'Brien. The Ambassador was still abed with the flu.

Somewhere along the way, Ellison of the Secret Service pressed me to know of the Reverend's movements after a courtesy visit to the embassy's Marine detail's Christmas party, less than two blocks away. Mr. Jackson was holding forth in the dining room. He informed me that he would spend some time at the Marine's party and then go to the Meridien Hotel to do a live network show beamed back to the States via satellite.

Will someone be with you? I was trying to find out if I was expected to go. The Secret Service was running out of gas and so was I.

Yes, Thelma and Bill said they'll go with me he replied.

I decided to split after the Marine party drop-in.

The Marine detail for our embassy in Damascus numbers less than a dozen. Seven men, three women and a Lieutenant Colonel in command. You would be surprised to learn that Jesse Jackson took over the Christmas party and turned it into a prayer service. After twenty minutes of mingling with the Marines and their Syrian guests, the lights were turned up. Jackson was introduced and he plunged immediately into the task of tying in the hope of Christmas with our mission in Syria. In a few minutes he was through. We joined hands and he prayed for the Marine detail and we departed.

One humorous incident with the media occurred as we left the embassy reception to which our press entourage was invited also. Ron Smothers, the *New York Times* correspondent and Jack White of *Time*

Magazine, both Black, were out of gas. In the short time that we had been together, I had earned a modest reputation of "Mr. Fixit." They approached me and expressed the desire to get back to the hotel.

Just tell your driver, I answered, thinking that would solve the dilemma.

That's the problem, complained Smothers, *he doesn't understand English.*

I remembered that Syria was once French. Maybe I could help them out and certify my international credentials at the same time to these big-shot newsmen. This was all in good-natured fun since they had been ribbing me about being a "slick preacher."

Take me to your driver, I said.

A few steps away, I could see the bewilderment on the face of a Syrian upon whom a strange language had been heaped by these two print jockeys.

Parlez vous Francaise, M'sieu?

Oui! Oui, M'sieu!

Conduize moi l'hotel Sheraton, sil vous plait?

Oui! Oui! he replied, his eyes twinkling.

Get in, Soul brothers! I commanded.

Both White and Smothers mouth were agape. I don't think they expected that from a Harlem preacher. Nor did they know that I had just exhausted my fluency in French (smile).

Back at the hotel, I busied myself getting ready for tomorrow's "program" as Khalil termed it. The first item of business was a visit to a refugee camp in response to Jackson's rquest. There was no word yet on the Assad meeting. There was an invitation from the Greek Catholic representative of the patriarch to attend a World Day of Prayer communion service in the evening. I would take it up with Jesse in the morning.

This was New Year's 1983. This was the first time in thirty-three years, Ann and I had not been together. It wasn't long before the blues had me. In five hours, the New Year would reach the east coast of the U.S. I set my alarm and called the overseas operator to reserve my call. Then I heard gunfire and laughed. I remembered that in the General Decorum memo, I had warned our delegation that in Syria there is a tradition of greeting the New Year with all kinds of firearms including machine guns. There would be no cause for alarm. As the shooting increased in intensity, I had to laugh again. HAPPY NEW YEAR, DAMASCUS!

Happy New Year

New Year's morning in Damascus found me awake at dawn. In a little while, the overseas operator called to tell me that it was impossible to get a circuit to the U.S. I really wanted to wish Ann a Happy New Year close to its beginning on the East coast. Maybe later, I thought.

After freshening up, since it was so early, I'd take breakfast in the coffee shop this morning. I was surprised to find Florence Tate and Tom Porter already there. The breakfast buffet was elegant and tasty. The pastries in the Mid-East are hard to beat.

The three of us tried to assess the previous day's activities without much definitive agreement. Neither of them had slept very well either. I attributed it to the first day's dizzying pace and the anxieties as to how our efforts were faring with the Syrians. We all agreed that the meeting with the religious leaders was the most grueling of all.

Tom Porter's analytical mind induced him to say, *Don't worry yet; we haven't seen Assad. He's the one who's going to decide whether to spring Goodman or not.*

I knew he was right.

Have you seen Khalil yet? Florence asked. She had these large brown innocent eyes of a little girl but I found out she could be tough if she had to. With all her skills in press relation, this was her first international experience. What a baptism of fire.

No, I answered. *He won't be here until about nine. It's not eight yet and I've got some personal business I must clear up with the Country Preacher.* Both of their heads jerked up simultaneously. They knew I had been upset about the press mess before the Goodman visit. They were as incensed as I was at the time. As they looked at me, I felt I had behaved like a good soldier the rest of the day, in spite of feeling embarassed publicly. With no further explanation, I made my way to 367.

The Reverend Jesse Louis Jackson was sitting up in his bed, wide awake. Eugene Wheeler was laying out his attire for the day.

May I speak to you, privately? I said ominously.

Jackson's eyebrow's arched high for a moment. *Gene, give us a couple of minutes, please.* he said softly.

I was prepared to leave Damascus on the next available flight. The exchange that took place in these few minutes does not need to be rehearsed in print. Suffice it to say, we settled it as Christian brothers. The Country Preacher promised me that it would never happen again. It hasn't.

I pushed back the sliding doors and yelled for Gene to finish what he had been doing and get filled in on today's program. I provided Jackson with the memo shown in Fig. 4. A comparison with the day's actual memo, Fig. 5, evidences the dynamics of how our mission functioned. Jesse readily agreed to the Communion service if it did not interfere with a chance to see President Assad.

Tom Porter arrived and with the briefing memo cleared, we made up the daily memo for distribution. It was now almost 8:30 a.m., time for me to meet Hadad. Porter took care of the memo while I started for the lobby.

Over Arabic coffee, Hadad with his ever present cigarette, told me there was yet no word on the proposed meeting with Assad and Khaddam. I mentioned to him the possibility of Jackson's meeting with the

Saudi ambassador. He nodded in a manner that I presumed met with his approval. At least he made no protest. The final detail was a little ticklish.

Justice for the Palestinian people is an issue dear to Jesse Jackson's heart and he has paid a woeful price for his support of their quest for a homeland. Through me, he had registered a desire to visit a Palestinian refugee camp. Both of us on separate missions had visited the Sabra and Shatilla camps in Lebanon three years earlier.* Hadad offered that the present division in the PLO made it too dangerous. As an alternate suggestion, arrangements had been made for a visit to a camp on the outskirts of Damascus, whose principal inhabitants were the displaced Syrians from the Golan Heights. I assured him this was a prudent measure.

It was settled. The Syrian refugee camp would be our first activity for this first Sunday in Damascus, 1984. At mid-day or thereabout, Jackson was scheduled to meet with the Saudi ambassador, then if it could be arranged, a chat with a member of the Syrian Parliament. At 12:30, after several attempts, I had a firm appointment for Inaan Raad, a member of the Lebanese Democratic National Front. Raad, I learned, had been the key contact in Jackson's initial meeting with Assad two years earlier. It was to our great advantage that Jackson was not meeting Hafez al-Assad for the first time. Raad was an important contact and fitted the profile of those who had "access to Assad."

The afternoon program at this juncture was unclear. I'd have to take my cue from Hadad; stay loose in case the Assad meeting was held today. If no word came by four, then we would surely make the Communion appearance. Besides, this was Sunday and

*The refugee camps of the 1982 massacres in Lebanon.

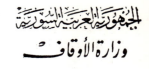

SUNDAY, 1 JANUARY 1984

CONFIRMED APPOINTMENTS

   9:20 A.M.   Departure/REFUGEE CAMP

   Displaced Syrians from Golan Heights

   11:30 A.M.   Saudi Ambassador to Syria

12 noon   Chairman , Syrian Parliament

      12:30   Inaan Raad/LEBANESE NATIONAL FRONT
         (suggested initial mtg wi ASSAD 1979)
            334 - 129

ON CALL FOR MTG WI FOREIGN MINISTER & PRESIDENT

4:45   DIVINE LITURGY

   His Holiness BISHOP ABOU MUHK

   (Sat to your left, head of table, center)
No response was made to this invitation; strong feeling
that it can now be ignored without offense

                    wyatt tee walker
         Chief,Protocol

Figure 4

66

DAILY MEMO

DATE 1/84   DAY SUNDAY

TODAY'S SCHEDULE

10:00 A.M.   REFUGEE CAMP
Displaced Syrians fr. Golan Heights
11:30 A.M.   SAUDI AMBASSADOR

12:00   CHAIRMAN, SYRIAN PARLIAMENT

DEPARTURE TIME FROM HOTEL 9:20 A.M.

RETURN TO HOTEL   11:30 A.M. *

Car Assignments Are Permanent for Duration of Mission

NO EXCEPTIONS

~~TOMARROW~~ THIS AFTERNOON ~~TONITE~~

5:00 P.M.   DIVINE WORSHIP. ST JOHN'S CHURCH
BISHOP ABU MWAK

* ON CALL TO FOREIGN MINISTRY/PRESIDENT

Figure 5

none of us had been to church.

In one of my infrequent personal visits to the Secret Service command post, I mentioned to the section chief in passing, the uncertainty of the meeting with the Foreign Minister and / or the President. I preferred not to appear chummy with them and felt for our purposes, I should keep them at a distance. I considered them "servants of the taxpayers." One agent, to whom I was not speaking, half-heard the intelligence I passed on to the chief. About a half an hour later, as I made my way through the third floor corridor, in preparation for our departure to the refugee camp, I overheard this same agent complaining that "that Rev. Walker is always giving the wrong information." Somehow he had passed on the information that the 10 a.m. destination was the Foreign Ministry.

Did I hear you call my name? There was cold steel in my voice.

Flustered by my unexpected appearance, he replied, *Yes. You don't give the right information.*

You're a expletive deleted liar. I bellowed. *I have never given the wrong information.* A small crowd was forming. *The information I give, is the information I get. If you did your job as well as I do mine, you wouldn't be a foot soldier. Where's your section chief?*

Whatever was going on in the command post of the Secret Service came to a screeching halt as I registered my formal protest and demanded an apology. I turned on my heel in my best Hollywood style. I did not know that this little episode would have grave repercussions the next day.

One of the things that stays fresh in my reminiscence about Damascus is that as serious as was our mission, there were always light moments at the oddest times. After we loaded up promptly at 9:45 for the visit to the refugee camp and Mr. Jackson was in place, we had our first "sightseeing" tour through central Damascus. It was a wild ride at 40 and 50 miles an hour. The bright sunny morning of this New Year's day seemed ripe with promise. That's when the humor struck.

Residential Damascus.

The logistics for this visit were very precise. At 10 a.m., our caravan of limousines, cars, weapons carriers and motocycle escort would be met at the entrance to the refugee camp by the camp's security chief and leader. Every refugee camp that I have visited, on the West Bank, in Lebanon, Jordan, wherever, has its own government and organization, including heavily armed security. For some inexplicable reason, the leader of the camp and his security were late in arriving at the agreed upon juncture. Consequently, we roared past the entrance and were two or three miles down the road before the motorcycle escort realized it had gone too far. That Sunday morning scene of confusion on this two lane Syrian road was a sight to behold. When the cars screeched to a halt, we all thought we had arrived and jumped out of our cars. Colonel Hisam, the burly chief of Syria's Political Security, was in the middle of the road gesticulating animatedly and speaking into a walkie-talkie. Our Secret Service was huddled around Jackson, protectively. By now the motorcycles were making a U turn, followed in uneven sequence by all the other cars in a hilarious display of non-coordination. Tires were screeching, sirens wailing and horns blowing. It was a real "Keystone Kop" caper.

After all the vehicles were turned around and the caravan re-assembled, we re-traced our route a couple of miles to the camp. Hisam, a section chief of the Secret Service and the head of the camp, after a quick huddle, determined that the entire caravan of cars would be permitted to enter. Fifteen hundred yards into the camp, all the cars stopped and we alighted and proceeded on foot.

Arrival at refugee camp.

Any visit to a refugee camp in the Mid-East is emotionally wrenching. Those of us from the West for

70

Camp security.

Faces in
refugee camp.

"V" for victory.

whom indoor plumbing and wall to wall carpeting is routine, undergo some form of culture-shock when you see raw sewage, a family of ten living in a one or two room hovel, the splotchy faces of the young certifying the poor nutrition and always — the presence of guns. Refugee camps in the mid-east are ravaged by external and internal terror, both physical and psychic. Most of the occupants have lived there for more than a generation; for the new generation, it is all they have ever known. There are more than two million Palestinian refugees who have been jarred loose from their homeland by the vagaries of war and geo-political immorality.* If the reader ever visits such a camp, your humanity can never be the same again.

This was not new ground for Jesse Jackson. He had been in refugee camps before. He gravitated immediately toward the children. That's where hope must be cultivated. He patted heads and picked up infants. The pre-teens gobbled up a small supply of Jackson's photos that Florence Tate had thoughtfully brought along. Soon, there were small scuffles for possession of the pictures and flashes of the "V" for victory signs for the benefit of the cameras. To Palestinians, it means a return to their homeland. I saw one newsman, camera down and face turned toward the wall. He was apparently not well.

Are you all right? I asked.

He was pale as a sheet. *I've seen a lot of things, but I wasn't prepared for this!* he confessed.

As we sped out of the camp compound nearly an hour later, I looked at the eager faces of the young and the weary eyes of the adults and mused that the human spirit is universal. Amidst all this squalor, the children were still smiling.

*See Mid-East essay, Appendix "G."

Good-bye!

Back at the Sheraton, what was to be a long afternoon, began to unfold with the news that the Saudi ambassador had cancelled but a member of the Syrian Parliament was in place and Inaan Raad was waiting. During these discussions another crucial turn of events was beginning to take shape.

As Hadad and I separated after our return from the refugee camp visit, he informed me that some pressing matters were going to have him occupied for an hour or two. He and his family would be eating New Year's dinner at the hotel.

Would you be good enough to join us?

I reasoned that if this Syrian gentleman wanted me to have dinner with his family, we were growing close, personally. I wanted to but I begged off with the promise to join them for dessert. He was gone five minutes, it seems, and I heard my name paged. At the house phone, Hamzeh Hamzeh was on the phone. Hadad instructed him to call me and arrange a meeting for 1:30 p.m.

That's ten minutes from now. It was 1:20 then.

I'll meet you in the lobby. I wondered what was up. This was my first dealings with Hamzeh.

After passing this development on to Mr. Jackson, I returned to the far end of the lobby and Hamzeh Hamzeh was already seated, smoking a cigaret and unsmiling.

He began to speak softly and matter-of-factly. *The meeting with the President will be tomorrow. All of the equipment of the news people must be gathered up now and taken to the presidential palace today for inspection.* Before I could ask, he quietly said, *Security.*

I called to his attention that Khalil and I had agreed on Saturday that four arms of the press would be present; one television crew, a print journalist, a magazine journalist, one color and one black and white photographer and Mr. Jackson's campaign photographer.

Hamzeh Hamzeh shook his head. Only four persons. I could sense this little man would not be harangued by any American. The other condition was a blow to Jackson's concern for his delegation. Everyone, ecumenical delegation and staff alike had paid their own way to Damascus. I had explained to Khalil on Saturday that it was Mr. Jackson's earnest desire to have all members "meet" Mr. Assad with the understanding that we would be immediately excused from any discussions led by the ecumenical team headed by Mr. Jackson. That included Howard, Mendelsohn and Tom Porter. During the next exchange, it was apparent that plan was down the tube.

Hamzeh Hamzeh informed me after the press pool matter was settled, that "two or three" would see the President. I insisted that the arrangement was for four persons. I unfolded the text of the cable invitation from Assad and pointed to the words "and whatsoever delegation you deem advisable." I continued pressing my point, largely bluffing. I sensed the Syrians were changing the rules on us.

I will not allow Mr. Jackson to be offended by this turn-about! I fumed with the intention of walking away in a huff after my last sentence was delivered. *We'll go back to the United States first!*

Before I could get to the last sentence, Hamzeh said softly, *One moment, I will call.*

In a few minutes he came back with the first real smile I had seen on him all day.

O.K. he held up four fingers. *Four.*

And to myself, I said, "Whew! That was close.

I made one more attempt to have Mr. Jackson's official photographer included but Hamzeh was adamant. Unfortunately, Julia Jones had to be scratched. The television people decided that two people could handle the assignment which would allow one color and one black and white photographer. These four were summoned to my room, 357 at 2 p.m. Michael Hartwell from *Time* magazine, Rick Lipski of UPI and a two man British crew to provide pool coverage for all three networks and Cable News Network. Christian Jacks would handle camera and Antoine de Maximy would be responsible for sound and light. Upon Florence's instructions, they brought with them all their gear, cameras, sound equipment, film, power packs, bags, etc. The equipment was then transported to the Palace for security check and overnight storage. The two still photographers complained that they would have no equipment with which to work during the interim. Hamzeh Hamzeh shrugged his shoulder and asked rhetorically,

Do you want to take pictures tomorrow? (the Jackson-Assad meeting?) There was no more complaint.

In a few minutes, I was back in Room 367 giving Jackson the latest word on the preparation for the meeting with President Hafez el-Assad. He seemed pleased and relieved that the meeting was definitely on, no matter what the restrictions. The media had been especially picky in their reports about the "on again – off again" proposed meeting with Assad. The real story was that it was never set until today and with all the preparations, no time had been discussed. We were satisfied that it was going to be sometime Monday since our scheduled departure was for mid-day Tuesday via Paris.

It was now near 3 p.m., Sunday, January 1st, 1984. The strain of waiting to hear from the Syrians on the Assad meeting was now moot. I shared with Jesse the interpersonal play that was taking shape between Hadad and myself. I suggested he take a break and after my *tete a tete* with Khalil's family, I would do likewise. There was time before the World Day of Prayer Communion service with the apostolic delegate of the Patriarch. The other members of the mission were released from "stand-by" status with instructions to use their free time as they chose but not to go anywhere alone. The only requirement was to meet at the St. John Church at 5:00 p.m.*

In a few minutes, I joined the Hadad family in the hotel restaurant. Mrs. Hadad is a beautiful dark-haired woman with carefully chiseled features and a complexion of bone china. She was as warm and gracious as Khalil with obvious pride in her family of two girls and a boy, all with dark hair but with Khalil's Mediterranean color. We shared a pleasant half-hour of conversation and picture-taking. Hadad reminded me that he would be joining Reverend Jack-

*See Fig. 6 at
end of chapter.

The Hadad family.

son and me at the service.

We arrived at the Church of St. John of Damascus just at five. This was the single instance that I rode with Mr. Jackson during our stay in Syria. It seems that our mission members were scattered all over Damascus. Prior to our leaving, I learned from Bruce Streathearn that Paganelli would also be in attendance. Bishop Abu Muhk greeted Reverend Jackson at the main entrance and the procession began. I remember being a little startled at how much news coverage there was for this religious service. The U.S. Ambassador and Mr. Jackson occupied the same pew, flanked on each side by Hadad and myself. Of course, Greek Catholic services are "high church" with considerable pageantry and burning of incense. A young people's choir sang several selections for the occasion. The service concluded with the celebration of Holy Communion in which all of us shared a com-

World Day of Prayer Commuion Service. (l-r, back row) Ellison, Theobald, Adair; (front row) Jackson, Paganelli, Walker, Howard, Hadad.

monality. It was quite a religious menagerie; the Country Preacher from Greenville, S.C., a Syrian diplomat, a Roman Catholic U.S. Ambassador and a Harlem preacher. "In Christ there is no east or west. . . ."

Back at the Sheraton, Jesse Jackson announced that it was New Year's and he'd like for everybody to eat dinner together.

We need to have a little fellowship.

His announcement was met with a chorus of "Amens" and "Right on." It was settled and the dinner hour was set for 7:30. I managed to slip away and call the states. The doors of the church were being opened when my call went through (that's the way Black Baptists refer to the moment in the service when new members are invited to give their lives to the Lord). I informed my assistant, Rev. Knight, that the meeting was on with Assad and to instruct the congregation to "pray mightily" that Goodman would be released. Somewhere in that busy Sunday, I talked to my wife and told her that I loved her.

My recollection is that our New Year's dinner was the most relaxed period of our stay in Syria. The meeting with Assad was firm, all the arrangements had been made, the saints were praying and it was a brand new year. Most of the Black members of the Fourth estate had attached themselves to our delegation on the strength of being "Soul Brothers," I guess. All in all, we had a nice time and as Chairman of the Board of Freedom National Bank, I picked up the check. The Country Preacher was profuse in thanking me for Freedom's generosity.

And now for tomorrow and Hafez al-Assad. When the New Year's dinner had ended, I thought my day was over. In my room, I brought my personal notes up to date. It has been my habit of late (since turning fifty) to make some historical record of the significant events of my involvement. A spin-off of this new habit is that I tend to collect memorabilia of all sorts. I have always regretted things I let slip through my fingers in the King days. Just when I had finished, a call came from Dr. Franklin Lamb who had traveled with the mission from Washington. Lamb held a Ph.D. in political science and was considered an expert on the Mid-East. He was with a friend who wanted very much to speak with Mr. Jackson. I glanced at my travel clock. It was almost twelve, midnight.

What's his name? I asked.

Labadi.

Who's he with?

He's not with anyone. He just feels it's important for him to see Reverend Jackson.

For some reason, this didn't seem to be right. I told Lamb I'd get back to him in ten minutes. I put on my slippers and went directly to Jackson's suite. The Country Preacher and three journalists were locked in a very talkative bid whist game. At a convenient break in the hilarity that seemed to overshadow the game itself, I made Jackson aware of the request. At the moment the name didn't ring a bell. Labadi is not an uncommon name in the Mid-East.

Check it out, buddy. With that, he returned to his bid whist game.

I decided to take matters into my own hands. I called Lamb and told him that Mr. Jackson wanted me to speak to this person first and then we'd go from there.

Where are you? He gave me a room number on the second floor and I told him I'd be right down. When Lamb answered my knock, it was then that I remembered who he was. I thought he was with the press corps. A very likable chap. Two steps into the room, I saw Labadi.

I know you! I blurted out. *Aren't you Mahmoud Labadi?*

I am. he replied.

We were together in Beirut, three years ago. I'm, Wyatt Walker.

Of course. You were with Dr. Jones* and the ministers.

We immediately embraced in Mid-East fashion with a soft kiss on each other's cheek. Mahmoud Labadi, administratively, was the no. 2 man in the PLO to Chairman Yasir Arafat. At one time they were inseparable. Mahmoud told me he was one of the casualties of the internal rift in the PLO and was for the present, living in Damascus.

There was no question in my mind that Jackson would want to see this man. If anyone had access to

*William A. Jones, pastor of Bethany Baptist Church in Brooklyn.

Assad, Mahmoud Labadi surely did.

It will take me a few minutes to clear this with the Secret Service and then I'll come back and bring you up personally. Having given this assurance, I was on my way back to 367.

I told the agents at Mr. Jackson's door, that in a few minutes, I would be escorting a visitor to Mr. Jackson's suite. Throughout our visit in Syria, the Secret Service posted two agents at Mr. Jackson's door twenty-four hours a day. Whenever anyone was entering, they turned the key which remained in the door all the time. If they didn't know you, you couldn't get in, period. At this instance, they asked was the guest a "Syrian citizen." I didn't know what kind of passport Mahmoud was carrying, so I just answered "Yes" to make it simple.

Mahmoud Labadi.

In a few minutes, Jackson and Labadi were locked in an enthusiastic embrace, kidding each other and talking over old times. In retrospect, this was an important meeting. Time magazine's January 16th issue credits Labadi with turning the tide with Assad. ". . .

he persuaded Mahmoud Labadi, a P.L.O. spokesman to present Jackson's case to P.L.O. faction leaders in Damascus. It was they who subsequently urged the Syrians to give up the flyer." My own view is that Time overstates the case but there is no gainsaying that Labadi is an important figure in Mid-East politics.

They must have chatted for quite a while; I stayed for an hour and then slipped away to 357 to get ready for Assad's day.

A l'occasion de la « Journée Mondiale de la Paix »

Les Chefs des Communautés Catholiques de Damas
ont l'honneur de vous inviter
à participer à la Divine Liturgie que présidera

Son Exc. Mgr. Nicola Rotunno
Pro - Nonce Apostolique

et célébrera

Mgr. François Abou Mokh
Vicaire Général Patriarcal Grec - Catholique

en l'Eglise St. Jean Damascène — Abou Raummaneh
le Dimanche 1 Janvier 1984 à 17 h.

Figure 6

The Day of Hafez al-Assad CHAPTER 5

The second day of 1984 was bright and sunny in Damascus, Syria. As was my routine, my first stop after breakfast was the suite of the Reverend Jesse Louis Jackson. He was down on the floor doing push-ups, a part of his daily regimen. I waited while he finished his set of push-ups and switched quickly to a set of sit-ups.

Wyatt, I want you to call Paganelli and see if he can see me this morning. he began. *If necessary, I'll come to him.*

"Uh-oh" I thought. "The pressure's getting to him." For me this was not a good sign, psychologically or tactically. We had been warned in the State Department briefing that we must support the U.S. ambassador and in no way abrogate his function as it related to the Goodman matter. I never felt that Paganelli was ever comfortable with our presence. He was in a very difficult position; Goodman was not now free; if he is released now, it will appear that there was something he didn't do. On the other hand, Jackson appeared to be turning to Paganelli for some help, some sort of carrot to strengthen his hand.

Bruce Streathearn was at his post down the hall, I literally sauntered in and mentioned that Mr. Jackson would like to see the Ambassador "if it could be arranged." I pretended to have something else pressing and told him I'd check back in a few minutes. I felt he needed to have privacy to make his call to the boss. When I started back toward the embassy command post, Bruce was coming to meet me.

What time, Wyatt? he asked.

Mr. Jackson would like to make it as soon as possible. I replied.

DAILY MEMO

DATE 2/84 DAY MONDAY

TODAY'S SCHEDULE

MEETING With FOREIGN MINISTER

"   "   PRESIDENT ASSAD

PLEASE NOTE: SOME RESTRICTIONS MAY PREVAIL
IN BOTH INSTANCES

DEPARTURE TIME FROM HOTEL 9:45 (TENTATIVE)

RETURN TO HOTEL NOON

Car Assignments Are Permanent for Duration of Mission

NO EXCEPTIONS

TOMORROW   THIS AFTERNOON   TONITE

PREPARE FOR EARLY MORNING
DEPARTURE!

Figure 7

Bruce was ahead of me. *If Reverend Jackson can come to the residence, the Ambassador will see him right away* was his rejoinder.

Before I returned to give Jackson the word, I alerted the Secret Service that "Mr. Jackson may have to run over to see the U.S. Ambassador for a few minutes.

At my report, Jackson started pulling on the trousers to his blue suit and told me to go get Tom Porter and Bill Howard. In short order, the three of them were on their way. It was not yet 8:30.

My anxiety about this early morning meeting was not certified until November of 1984. When Mr. Jackson returned in about thirty minutes, he did not volunteer to me the nature of the meeting nor did I ask. Back in the States, though in his company more than fifty times, I never thought to ask. In November, Bill Howard and I were enroute to Kennedy airport to meet Inaan Raad who was visiting the U.S. I was then in the midst of putting together a manuscript for this book and I shared with Howard my thoughts about that meeting with Paganelli. Howard confirmed my suspicions that Jackson was looking for some help that Paganelli could not give. The specifics of that meeting must remain confidential but suffice it to say, that though Jackson was not successful in what he proposed, the ultimate release of Goodman without Paganelli's assistance, enhanced his prowess in international affairs.

The hours between Jackson's return from the Paganelli meeting and the departure for the Assad meeting dragged by. There was nothing really to do. It was too early to pack and the uncertainty hung heavy on everyone connected with the mission. Khalil Hadad had come to the hotel about 10:00 a.m. to let me know that the meeting with Assad would be at 1:00

p.m. Departure time from the hotel would be promptly at 12:30. He stressed that the meeting with President Assad would be "30 minutes at the most." It
would be best if at the end of the thirty minute discussion, Mr. Jackson would make the move to end
the conversation. Assad's health, he explained, was a
factor in deciding on the strict regimen. We agreed
readily not wanting to impair our host's convales-
cence* or raise his ire. Now it was just a matter of
hanging tough until the Jackson-Assad meeting was a
reality.

Finally, the bewitching hour was upon us. At noon,
the entire mission gathered in Jackson's suite. Not
much was said formally, nor was there any necessity
for anything much to be said. Everyone knew this
was *it*. The Country Preacher was very low key. He
seemed hopeful and resigned. I suppose, that whatever the outcome, we had given this proposition our
best shot. Everything else was in the Lord's hands.

No one was prepared for the sudden surprise sprung
on us by the Syrians. The Secret Service went into
shock. It all began when the agent with whom I had
had the "theological" discussion Sunday morning
tried to get some revenge. The discussion team led by
Jackson included Tom Porter, Bill Howard and Jack
Mendelsohn. Howard and Mendelsohn would ride
with Jackson which made Tom Porter the odd man
out. The adversary agent was standing at the rear of
Mr. Jackson's limousine. He was the nearest agent at
hand and I was respecting the detail's imposed re-
striction of "two passengers only" with the Reverend. The importance of today's meeting caused me to
set aside my personal differences.

I'll need a car for Mr. Porter, I said civilly, if not
politely.

*Assad suffered a serious heart
attack earlier in '83.

86

He snarled his reply. *Find a car!*

"Keep your cool, Harlem Preacher," I told myself.

In a moment, I put Tom Porter in my regular car. By the time I took a dozen steps back to the curb to Jackson's limo, all of the Secret Service agents were moving to and fro like an old time movie.

Someone shouted, *The Syrians say we can't go!*

If WE don't go, REVEREND JACKSON doesn't go. another shouted in return.

I had never seen this agent before.

You are in no position to make that decision, I shot back as I reached for the back door of Jackson's limousine. The 'adversary agent' put his hand on the door in an effort to keep the door closed. All the chips were down so far as I was concerned. I nearly yanked that door off its hinges into the knees of 'my friend.'

What's going on Wyatt? Jesse yelled.

They (the Secret Service) say if they can't go, you don't go. JESSE, THIS IS WHAT WE CAME TO DAMASCUS FOR! I said with all the toughness I could muster in these few seconds.

Secret service "flap".

To his honor and glory, Jackson never hesitated. *I know you're right!* he said climbing out of the car. *How will we get there?*

They (the Syrians) *have a white Cadillac right over there.* All of the above exchange took place in less than a minute's time. As I ushered the Leader and his small retinue to the white Cadillac, ten paces away, the unfamiliar agent who made the pronouncement that Mr. Jackson was not going, was at my elbow trying to dissuade me from putting Jackson into the Syrian car.

Wait a minute, we'll negotiate leaving our weapons . . .

I cut him off in mid-sentence. *Fine, Mr. Jackson can sit in this car while you work on it.*

He protested. *But the Syrians might take him away . . .*

You don't need to worry; Mr. Jackson's safe with the Syrians. It's some of you I worry about! Iago* would have been proud of that stiletto thrust.

We can't go! This was the voice of Colonel Hisam, chief of Syria's Political Security. He was speaking to other agents who were now desperately trying to salvage something from a bad situation. I pieced together in the moments following the disappearance of the white Cadillac behind the motorcycle escort, that for this meeting, Assad's presidential security police were in charge. To say that they were in charge was the understatement of this young year.

The detail of Secret Service agents remained in front of the hotel for almost a half-hour. They had to be embarassed. They complained, legitimately, that they should have known before learning of the restrictions at curbside.

*A character in William Shakespeare's *Othello*.

We wouldn't have done that to them in America griped one of the agents.

Back in Jackson's suite, I was rehearsing the curbside drama for the rest of the mission, when Dwight Ellison came in. He was very somber and was accompanied by this "unfamiliar" agent. He asked could they see me privately. I followed into the corridor. Ellison turned to me and asked,

Do you mind going to my room?

Not at all. I wondered if I was under arrest or something.

Ellison advised me in the presence of this other agent, that there had been what amounted to a "technical violation" of their trust since Reverend Jackson had elected to go without them. All of this could be straightened out if he, (Ellison) could see Reverend Jackson immediately upon his return *BEFORE* he talked to anyone. I assured him that it would be arranged.

He then shared with me the details of the "technical violation" of the Service's duty. It could all be repaired if Reverend Jackson would agree to sign two documents they would prepare.

Is that it? I asked anxious to rejoin the other mission members.

That's it. Ellison replied.

Then the "unfamiliar agent" spoke as I started for the door.

I'd like to introduce myself to you, Dr. Walker. I'm Patrick Miller. I'm in charge of the Secret Service detail here in Syria.

I turned to look him straight in the eye. *How is it that I'm just meeting you now?* I asked icily.

Well, I like to keep a low profile. I want you to know that I meant no offense downstairs. Just trying

to do my job.

We shook hands but it struck me as odd practice that his profile was so low that I had never seen him until today. Out in the corridor, Ellison allowed that after they had simmered down, they all agreed that if they had been in Reverend Jackson's shoes, they would have done the same thing. *Ciao!*

In suite 367, after an hour had elapsed, we all began to look for the Leader. The time restrictions imposed meant he'd have to be back around two o'clock. Two-thirty passed, no Jesse! Three o'clock; no Jesse! The room began to resemble the wake of a funeral.

Get your heads up, darlins'. I cajoled. *You know my jury theory.*

Sunday afternoon, as the day wore on, the non-information about the Assad meeting induced one of our band to remark. *These Syrians are moving too slow!* It was then that I reminded them that when a man is on trial for his life, the longer the jury stays out, the better chance he has.

Let the jury take its time. Don't worry, the Lord is in it!

When the Country Preacher had not returned at 3:30, I guessed that Assad had extended the meeting. If so, that would be a terrific sign.

At 3:40, we could hear the sirens in the distance. I raced to the lobby, anxious to get a reading on what had transpired *and* to get the Secret Service matter repaired. The Assad meeting group returned in a *black* limousine. "Nice touch." I thought. I gave Jackson a pre-arranged sign, signifying that I needed to talk to him right away.

Inside the elevator, I told him Dwight (Ellison) needed to see him immediately in private. Ellison was waiting with Miller at the third floor landing.

Once inside the suite, we pushed past the sliding doors into Jackson's bedroom. The quick run-down on the situation I gave the Country Preacher was sufficient for him to sign the documents prepared by the Service without hesitation. The full text appears below:

Damascus, Syria
January 2, 1984

Mr. John R. Simpson
Director
United States Secret Service
Washington, D.C.

Dear Mr. Simpson:

This is to confirm that, at 12:30 pm local time (10:32 am GMT) this date I orally advised Inspector Patrick Miller, U.S. Secret Service, that I no longer required or desired the protection of the U.S. Secret Service which was instituted, on order of Secretary of the Treasury Donald Regan, on November 10, 1983.

In making the decision, I absolved the U.S. Secret Service of any and all responsibility relative to my physical security.

Jesse L. Jackson

Damascus, Syria
January 2, 1984

The Honorable Donald T. Regan
Secretary of the Treasury
Washington, D.C.

Sir:

Pursuant to the Public Law which authorized my being provided with physical security by the U.S. Secret Service on November 10, 1983, I hereby request that such protection be reinstituted, effective 3:00 p.m., January 2, 1984.

Jesse L. Jackson

The net effect was that the Secret Service was "off the hook" and security for Mr. Jackson was restored. In reflection, I think Jesse was on such a "high" from the meeting with President Assad that he would have signed anything at that point (smile).

It should be no surprise to the reader that as I write this account, Jesse Jackson has already been on NBC's Saturday Night Live! Everyone, but "the Family" was dismissed from the suite. Jackson, quickly, in animated detail described how the "30 minute" meeting with Assad was extended to another 30 minutes, at which point, the President told the aide who had twice interrupted the discussions not to come back until he sent for him.

I think we all felt, "Wow!"

Since I was not privy to the Assad meeting directly, Bill Howard's digest of that meeting appears now for first-hand evidence.

> When the two cars pulled away from the Damascus Sheraton Hotel, it felt a bit strange because for the first time since our arrival in Syria we were not under secret service escort. Instead, we were being driven to the residence of President Asaad by representatives of the Syrian government. Jesse Jackson and I were in a white Cadillac with two Syrian men and we were being followed by a Mercedes Benz which had as its passengers Tom Porter and Jack Mendlesohn.
>
> We had no idea where we were headed, but quickly we found ourselves in the suburbs of Damascus, riding along a country road where a lot of new apartment construction was in progress. For quite a few miles we drove parallel to a railroad that was being protected by heavily armed men who lay beside the tracks couched behind sub-machine guns as if to protect the railroad from sabotage. Our escorts spoke only Arabic, but I sensed that Rev. Jackson presumed they understood English. So, we were very quiet, speaking only occa-

sionally about superficial things, like the scenery. All together our ride to President Asaad's villa took about one half hour, but the trip seemed to be taking longer than it actually did. We saw many people walking along the country roads, sometimes carrying large loads. There was an occasional suburban residence that appeared quite luxurious from the road. So at the sight of each such place, I would surmise, perhaps this is the place we were going. From time to time, the drivers would slow down and pull over to the side of the road, speaking into walkie-talkies. I decided later that we were moving along a bit ahead of our schedule, and it is correct protocol to arrive exactly on time when visiting the head of state. We reached Asaad's villa as the clock struck two. It was modest-looking place, surrounded by a high wall. The gates were flung open at the moment we arrived, and as we exited the car we saw the Syrian President walking across the lawn with a big smile and a spry gait. I was a bit surprised by this because there had been much talk about his failing health before we left the States. He seemed like a very robust man, quite well dressed, although tasteful and quiet. And his villa, while clearly elegant, could also be considered on the simple side for a man of his obvious power.

Asaad greeted those of us who accompanied Rev. Jackson with equal warmth. He escorted us all into what appeared to be his study just off a well-appointed patio, and without much formality, we began immediately to engage in substantive discussion. Much of what Asaad talked about had to do with his regret that US-Syria relations had fallen to such a sad state. He repeatedly stated that Syria had nothing to gain by having poor relations with the US and he applauded some of the steps which the Carter Administration had taken to help ease Middle East tension. He even spoke favorably about a visit which Jimmy Carter had paid him as a private citizen following his term in the White House. Without question, he reserved his harshest words for the Israel-Lebanon peace treaty, saying that it was a fundamental compromise of Lebanese sovereignty. What was perhaps most notable about the atmosphere of the meeting was the obvious regard in which Mr. Asaad held Jesse Jackson, and I had the distinct impression that, were it not for this high regard, we would not have been sitting there.

After repeated interruptions to mark the established time of our meeting, and in each instance having Mr. Asaad direct his aides to allow us to continue, after 90 minutes we concluded our discussion. Mr. Asaad commited to appeal to his Council of Ministers to reconsider their policy regarding the release of Goodman. Rev. Jackson remained behind for a few extra minutes for a private chat with Mr. Asaad before we were returned to our hotel.

Just as we had been driven by white Cadillac going to Mr. Asaad's home, we returned in a black Cadillac. I presumed this was for security reasons.

We were all visibly encouraged by the conversations with Mr. Asaad, although we were given no firm assurance of what the outcome would be. At least, the answer was not a definitive no. Jesse Jackson appeared positive but clearly not certain, so he was a bit restrained. And as we had been enroute to Mr. Asaad's villa, we remained relatively quiet during the ride back to the hotel. The return trip seemed to have gone much faster as it is frequently the case when one knows one's destination.

The reader must appreciate that by now, the assembled media was in a frenzy. Jackson hurriedly prepared a brief statement which was absolutely non-committal. He did allude to the fact the conversation was extended and President Assad had assured him that he would convene the appropriate leadership to reconsider Jackson's appeal. We did not know at this point in time that the military high command had met the night of our arrival (Friday) and had decided that Goodman should remain a prisoner.

The press briefing ended with Mr. Jackson's disclosure that he expected to have some word from

President Assad "sometime this evening." Our scheduled departure now was on a Lufthansa flight to Frankfurt and then on to New York via Pan Am. There really wasn't anything to do now but wait and pray.

Back in 367, Jackson was ebullient. For a second time, he rehearsed the "private" discussion he held with Assad without the interpreter.

He told me he hoped he was going to have a successful meeting. I told him 'Presidents and pastors are very much alike; they have very few unsuccessful meetings' and then we did a lot of back-slapping and hee-hawing like colored folks do.

None of us were absolutely sure this was an historical account. If so, we knew Jesse Louis Jackson had embellished it just a wee bit (smile).

The suggestion was suddenly made that since we wouldn't be hearing from the President for several hours, this would be a splendid opportunity for us to visit the world famous Souk Al-Hamideh market.

When informed of the plans, Ellison said there was no way they could provide adequate security in the Souk.

That's the most vulnerable place in Damascus, he lamented.

The Leader wants to go. This is he and Jackie's (Mrs. Jackson) wedding anniversary. He wants to pick up a gift. Come on, you guys are pros, right!

I could tell he didn't like the idea but in a little while, it was all arranged. Ellison recalled that when Jimmy Carter had visited Damascus, that an anti-American riot almost erupted because they went to the Souk in full caravan. In this instance, Jonathan and Jesse Jr. would ride with their father and the Secret Service would only have one vehicle with which to contend and cause less attention. The rest of us would go to the Souk on our own. Since this was not an "official" but rather a recreational exercise, I suspended all car assignments.

Tom Porter, Florence Tate and I found ourselves as car-mates. I have visited the bazaars of the Casbah in Tangiers, the Khan el Khalil of Old Cairo, the Iron Market of Port au Prince, the Old City in Jerusalem, the Peoples Market in Dakar. Each has its own character and charm. But the Souk in Damascus near the Street called Straight* is an experience every traveler will cherish. I wanted badly to see the Street called Straight (I missed it) and bring a souvenir to my bride of thirty-three years. This would soften the effect of my absence at holiday time, I hoped.

Souk al-Hamideh.

The Souk Al-Hamideh, completed in 1883, affords an adventure to the eager shopper. The best way to see the Souk is to enter through the main entrance and walk straight down the wide main street. The

*Acts 9:11

96

corrugated iron roof allows ribbons of sunlight in through its stones and bullet holes. A maze of narrow streets and alleys leading off both sides of the main street introduces you to the various smaller souks where specific goods (leather, rugs, spices, wood, cutlery and gold) are displayed for sale.

The Omayyad Mosque is at one edge of the Souk. It was of particular interest because of the legend that John the Baptist's head is buried beneath it. It is a sight to behold. The Omayyad Caliphate (Arab empire) stretched from India across Persia, Syria, all of northern Africa to Spain. Damascus became its capital and this mosque dates to that period (636 A.D.).

Omayyd Mosque.

This was our first venture away from the hotel other than on official business. There had been no opportunity for us to gauge the reaction of the general population of Damascus to our visit. This visit to the Souk provided us with some valuable insight. After Tom and I finished our brief shopping and visited the

Omayyad Mosque, an earlier experience, provoked us to visit some shops at random to take a mini-Gallup poll. In the first shops we entered, the proprietor either quietly or very openly said "Yacksun! Viva la America! " or something comparable. The cameras around our necks and Black countenances betrayed our identities immediately. We must have visited twenty shops in that last hour in the Souk and without exception, every shopkeeper knew who we were and applauded our efforts to free Goodman. Several were very verbal even to the point of expressing the sentiment, "We want to be friends with America." or

Scene in "Souk".

"Do not push us into the arms of the Soviets." Back at the Sheraton, other members disclosed that they had a similar experience. Guess who we bumped into around dusk in the Souk in Damascus? Jesse Louis Jackson, the Country Preacher from Greenville, South Carolina (smile).

On the way back to the hotel, considerably after dark, our driver seemed to be taking the wrong route to the hotel. *Where are we going?* I asked in English, fully aware that he spoke only Arabic. He gestured "up" and pointed to his eyes. Then I remembered that Khalil, on one occasion, mentioned that before I left Syria, I should see Damascus by night from the mountains above the city. What a thoughtful gentleman. Somehow, he had found time to instruct my driver to give me a chance to see that spectacular view. The lights of the city sparkled like diamonds on a large black velvet cloth. Elven hundred feet above one of the world's oldest cities, I wondered what tomorrow might bring. My thoughts were interrupted by our driver saying insistently, *Sheraton, Sheraton!* and pointing in the direction of our hotel. Indeed, we could make out the configuration of our hotel. Before too long, we were making our way across the lobby to the elevators and Room 367.

There was some considerable admiration for the huge brass salver that I purchased for my wife and quite a few laughs at the Syrian hats Tom and I were wearing. We all had a lot of fun reviewing each other's souvenirs. Soon talk of dinner began to invade our conversations. I decided to eat with Ed Theobald from New Hampshire. I told him I didn't want him to think I was anti-Catholic. It was nearly eight o'clock Monday evening, January 2, 1984. Halfway through our meal, Farrakhan and Akbar Muhammed joined us in the hotel restaurant. Other members of the mission were scattered around the restaurant eating dinner also.

Any word yet from the President?

Reagan isn't going to call, Louis responded, kiddingly. *He knew I meant President Assad.* Then seriously, he said, *We just came by Jesse's room. There's no word yet. He say's he's going to take a nap if he can.*

Theobald made a dinner recommendation to Farrakhan and Muhammad and the rest of the meal was finished in small talk. A little after nine, Bill Howard came in shirt-sleeves. This was out of character for him.

Jesse wants to see everybody in his suite right away!

The restaurant emptied of our mission members forthwith. Our sudden exodus did not go unnoticed. The press knew something was up. Upstairs in the suite, Jackson who appeared as if he might have had a cat-nap, was sitting in the salon area of the suite, clad only in slacks, slippers and a "T" shirt. His countenance was a little somber and intense. The ebullience was gone.

I just received a call from the secretary to the President and he has requested that we delay our departure tomorrow morning.

I heard Gene Wheeler gasp, *Oh my God!* It was Gene Wheeler who had the thankless task, among other things, to collect passports, organize luggage and alter travel plans for the fifty-four persons in our entourage (mission members, Secret Service and press corps). He had just finished switching our route from Paris to Frankfurt. The next commercial flights by any route would be Thursday!

My recollection is that there was no dissenting opinion that if Assad wanted us to stay over another day, it had to be of prime importance. Of course we had to consider that if we got a turn-down, we'd have to spend another day or so in Damascus with our heads down – so to speak. The whole process of finalizing the decision to stay could not have taken more than an hour at the most. We had been at stand-by on packing our bags, etc. and Wheeler, in light of this new development, instructed everyone to continue to "stand-by."

We could be here for a couple a more days he remarked with resignation.

We are going to have to do something about the press. They want to know something. Florence chimed in almost apologetically.

Jackson turned to Bill Howard. *Bill, you and Wyatt and whoever, frame up a brief statement for me, one page. Florence, inform the press we'll have a briefing in an hour.*

Let's do this over coffee, Wyatt, Howard suggested. Then he announced, *Anyone who wants to help with this, meet us in the restaurant coffee shop.*

I chuckled when I saw Howard later on. He had put his coat and tie on. He really was a formal fellow but what a gentleman. It seemed incredible that he had once been my student during a teaching tenure at Princeton Seminary in the early seventies. We were joined shortly by Thelma Adair, Florence Tate, Porter and Theobald. Strangely enough, no effort was made at first to prepare the statement. There was unanimous agreement that Jesse Jackson did not need to meet the press anymore this day. In our view he was media-saturated. The prevailing opinion was that even with the prepared statement, if Jackson were present, the questions would be inevitable. Some chance remark could risk an awkward situation with the Syrians. Besides, we were all tired of the way the media had been badgering Jesse. The bottom line was, at this point, that there was nothing new to say except at the request of Assad, we would be delaying our departure period.

Does anyone have a suggestion? Bill Howard asked.

I spoke right up. *Bill, you have said I'm not bashful*

and I'm not. I really think what we ought to do is to have Florence open the press briefing and announce we have a prepared statement from Mr. Jackson; his protocol officer, Wyatt Walker, will read it and there will be no questions. I'm volunteering because of my experience with the media and because I'm tough. They're going crazy. At this point we're going to have to control them and not allow them to control us.

Thelma Adair responded, *I think that's a splendid idea and Wyatt can handle it.*

By this time, two or three other members of the mission had entered the restaurant and pulled up chairs. There was general agreement on our course of action and the only detail remaining was to inform Jesse Louis Jackson.

I'll take care of that, Bill Howard said firmly. *You guys get the statement together.*

While Howard went up to the suite to inform the Leader, two or three of us knocked out the statement in quick order. I typed it up on my Brother EP-22 and cleared it with Jackson. Howard had reported that he was comfortable with our approach and he was going on to bed.

On the way to the briefing room, Howard asked me, *Are you going like that?* With the delay, I had no fifth shirt, so I had donned a black turtleneck over which I slipped a white tuxedo shirt with all those frills. I didn't get a chance to wear it for the embassy reception.

Sure thing, I replied. *This is only going to take a hot minute.*

The full complement of the media was in attendance for the briefing. All the networks, CNN, the wire services, Reuters, etc. Florence, a little shakily, made her announcement as planned. At *There will be no questions*, there was considerable groaning. The nostalgia of the King days swept over me as I began reading the statement. It was like old times, again.

Statement of Jesse Jackson

Damascus, Syria
January 2, 1984

Today, as you know, we met for one and one half hours with President Assad. It was a warm and meaningful meeting. He has heard our moral appeal to release Lt. Robert Goodman on humanitarian grounds as a way to relieve tension and break the cycle of pain. There is obviously great concern about the combat posture and reconnaisance flights, but President Assad is keenly aware of the emerging atmosphere in the USA expressed by the three former CIA Directors, Turner, Colby and Schlesinger, Senator Goldwater and Vice President Mondale.

My own assessment is that neither nation has a vested interest in escalating war tensions. President Assad has currently convened the appropriate leadership and our appeal is being deliberated upon. These deliberations are signs of hope.

Thus we have responded to an official request just moments ago to delay our departure on Lufthansa's 8:20 a.m. flight tomorrow and I will necessarily withhold any further comment because we are at a very sensitive stage of the developments.

Please be assured that the media will be advised promptly of the result of our meeting with a high Syrian official tomorrow morning.

The instant I finished the statement, a torrent of questions came at me. I stood up and as politely as I could, said *Thank you very much* and strode toward the exit.

A voice with a pronounced British clip shouted, *Come on m____r f____r, you've got to give us more than that!*

The Holy Spirit helped me to continue walking without even turning my head to see where this obscenity came from. Florence reported to me later that the room was in bedlam.

Those who had not attended the briefing gathered immediately in the coffee shop for a post-mortem on our press ploy. We gave ourselves high marks in spite of the untoward conduct of the Reuters correspondent (Florence identified him for me). All of a sudden, Jackson appeared with a broad smile on his face.

Akbar (Muhammed) is giving my mission a bad name. I heard all the way upstairs that after the press briefing, he took the Reuters man over in a corner in the lobby and told him he didn't appreciate him speaking to Wyatt the way he did. Muhammed stands six-two and is 230 pounds of coiled muscle; he is one of the princes of the celebrated Fruit of Islam, the Nation's Security Division. *Then he told him, if he didn't seek Wyatt out and beg his pardon, he was going to introduce him to an old fashioned American ass-kicking.*

The whole mission broke up with laughter.

I suppose it was nearly mid-nite before our informal gathering broke up. For me it was bedtime and I wanted to get a good night's sleep. There was so much uncertainty about tomorrow – I wanted to be ready.

Wyatt! It was the Country Preacher calling. *You and someone need to get with the Secret Service and explore how we're going to get out of here. We might as well act as if Goodman is going to be released. If he isn't, we'll be here until Thursday, anyhow.*

O.K. I answered. *Come on Minister Farrakhan. You and Akbar can help me with this.*

Upstairs, at the Secret Service command post, I learned that Ellison's detail was on duty; he had just gone on "break." I told his deputy that it was fairly important for me to see him right away and I wouldn't keep him very long. I'd be in the embassy headquarters down the hall.

While we were waiting for Ellison, I explored with Bruce Streathern, the possibility of getting a military transport into Damascus. Pat O'Brien volunteered that if we could get clearance from the Syrian government, he could have one on the ground in four hours. I was confident we would have an answer by ten and clearance by noon – that is, if we get the *right* answer at ten o'clock.

It wasn't very long before Ellison arrived with Patrick Miller. I announced the agenda and Miller immediately deferred to Ellison to carry the ball for Service. Ellison outlined the options available so far as he knew: Syrian Airlines or Assad's private 727. None of the agents wanted to fly Syrian Airlines because of the recent history of hi-jackings and terrorism; maintenance of their equipment was no small problem either. The greatest reservation was the potential of being shot down by Israeli jets! If the Reverend flies Syrian Airlines, they would have to go, but they'd rather not.

The second option was more attractive. Assad's personal 727 was the next thing to Air Force One in maintenance and competency of crew. No problem so far as the service was concerned if President Assad made his personal jet available.

Suppose Reverend Jackson requests permission for

an American military transport to land in Damascus?
I interjected.

That would be the best of all possible worlds. Ellison responded.

This session closed as quietly as it had opened. We
said good-night to each other and went to our rooms. I
checked by Room 367 and left word with Gene
Wheeler that my assignment was completed. The
Rev. Jesse Louis Jackson was sound asleep. I continued on to my room wondering if tomorrow would
indeed be THE DAY OF RELEASE.

The Day of Release

CHAPTER 6

Wednesday morning, January 3rd was a gray overcast day. I made a few notes for future historical purposes (this narrative is one result) before going to
breakfast. at 8:15, I was in the Leader's suite clearing
the DAILY MEMO which was the most uncertain of
our entire stay. The President's secretary had promised on last evening that we would hear from a "high
government official" by 10:00 a.m. There wasn't any
move that could be made until that call came
through.

I slid the door open to Jackson's bedroom. He was
sitting up reading.

Good morning, Leader, I greeted him.

How ya' making it, Brother Wyatt? he returned.

I mentioned that if the memo was O.K., I'd slip it
under everyone's door and then check out the lobby
to see if anything was happening.

As I wandered through the lobby, I caught a glimpse
of my counterpart and new friend, Khalil Abu Hadad.

I was just looking for you, he said. *Can Reverend
Jackson be in the Foreign Minister's office at 10
o'clock?*

Let me run upstairs and see, I responded with outward calm. My heart began to race. On the elevator, I
muttered, *What's taking this damn elevator so long?*
At the third floor landing, I vaulted out of my brass
cage like Carl Lewis out of the starting blocks for the
hundred yard dash. I zipped past the command post of
the U.S. embassy staff without a glance. A member of
the Secret Service detail who was familiar with my
"cool" called to me.

What's up Reverend? as I continued on to 367. The
agent at the door was already turning the key. In I

DAILY MEMO

DATE 3/84 DAY **TUESDAY**

T O D A Y ' S   S C H E D U L E

10:00 A.M. GENERAL ALERT #367 *

FINAL PRESS BRIEFING BY NOON!

ALL PERSONAL ACCOUNTS MUST BE CLEARED BEFORE PRESS BRIEFING

DEPARTURE TIME FROM HOTEL ___

RETURN TO HOTEL ___

Car Assignments Are Permanent for Duration of Mission

NO EXCEPTIONS

T O M O R R O W   T H I S   A F T E R N O O N   T O N I T E

STANDBY FOR INFO

* ALL BAGGAGE TO BE CHECKED MUST BE READY BY THIS TIME. ALL OTHERS MUST BE READY, IF NECESSARY BY NOON

Figure 8

108

burst, my face lit up like a Christmas tree. The sliding door to Jackson's bedroom was to my right. I stopped and pulled the door almost closed. Jesse Louis Jackson looked up, not startled but not casually either. He had been immersed in reading one of the several documents that Tom Porter turned out every day.

Leader, I began conspiratorially, *can you be in the Foreign Secretary's office at ten?*

His eyes widened and he shot back, *If I need to be.* He was wide awake but still in his skivvies.

You need to be! I said confidently and with the air that this was "the Biggie."

Immediately, the Country Preacher from Greenville, South Carolina began to dress. I left through the rear door of Jackson's suite and roused Bill Howard and Tom Porter. I told Howard to get Jack Mendelsohn. Back up the corridor I sped. At the Secret Service command post, I stuck my head in the door and informed them that Mr. Jackson would be leaving for Khaddam's office at 9:55 sharp! No one was in the embassy office, so I continued on to the elevator to let Hadad know all systems were "Go."

I informed Khalil that everything was in place for the 10:00 a.m. meeting; he responded by saying to me:

Dr. Walker, I think you should go to the meeting this morning. His manner was very confidential. Sunday evening, when I saw him last, I gingerly pressed to get some clue as to what today's verdict might be. In no way did I want him to breach his confidentiality, but the suspense was killing me. He must have been aware of what I was trying to do. His only response was that he felt there would be some "good news" tomorrow. This seemed to be the confirmation. He wanted me to be there!

I'll have to clear that with Mr. Jackson, I said. I did an instant replay of my earlier dash to the Jackson suite.

Leader, I began, *Hadad says I should go this morning.*

I think that's a splended idea, he replied.

I must say, I'm delighted that I may go, was my quick reply.

Tom Porter and I rode in our regular car. Florence Tate and Julia Jones rode with us since the full complement of the media was right on our heels. *This is going to be historic*, Florence squealed.

I offered that I thought Assad was going to tell us that he would release Goodman ten days from now. It was too much to expect Assad to turn him over to us today. All of a sudden, I realized we had been riding longer than necessary to reach the Foreign Ministry building. The neighborhood through which we were passing was altogether unfamiliar.

Do you think we're being kidnapped, Tom? I asked.

Hell no. Who would pay the ransom for us, he grumped. *These cats are just lost.*

We were now ascending a steep hill. Our caravan of cars were just poking along and the sirens were silent.

I know what it is. We're too early and they're just riding around to kill some time, I suggestsed. That guess turned out to be exactly correct.

The cars speeded up, made a "U" turn and in a few minutes we were being ushered into the private first floor offices of Abdel Halim Khaddam, Foreign Secretary of the Republic of Syria. Khaddam was seated in front of his desk at a right angle. The interpreter was to his right, and then Tom Porter. Jesse Louis Jackson the Country Preacher from Greenville, South Carolina, sat opposite Khaddam, flanked on his left by Howard, Mendelsohn and myself.

My throat was dry and my heart was pulsating like the sound of a runaway freight train. The photo opportunity for the media was at an end. Somehow, Florence Tate and Julia Jones had managed to remain while the rest of the media people were dismissed. They stood a discreet distance away from the "discussion group."

The small talk between Jackson and Khaddam had awkwardly run out. It was 10:11 a.m., Tuesday, January 3, 1984. The atmosphere in the Secretary's office was tense, if not electric. The pace since our arrival was either dizzying or maddening; too fast or too slow. In this moment it seemed as if time had been suspended, frozen.

Final meeting with Khaddam.

The offical interpreter began. *Mr. Jackson, the meeting this morning will be a brief one.*

I thought to myself, "The decision has been made. This is it!" For some inexplicable reason, I had always been optimistic. I kept telling the others, *Don't worry, the Lord is in it.* I was convinced I saw

God working in Jesse's life in much the same manner that I had seen Him working in Martin's twenty years earlier.

The interpreter continued . . . *President Assad has asked me to inform you that on the basis of your moral appeal . . .*

I WAS READY TO SCREAM!

. . . we shall release to you Lt. Goodman.

For a millisecond, this scenario seemed unreal. I was convinced that the American media and a large segment of the American public including some critical Blacks, were poised, expecting Jesse to fall on his face. The most improbable players in this international drama were a Black Baptist preacher from Greenville, South Carolina and an alleged strong-armed Arab dictator. In this single instant, it seemed that Jesse Louis Jackson had accomplished the impossible.

Lt. Robert O. Goodman, the Black naval navigator/bombadier had been shot down in the Chouf mountains while on a reconnaisance and bombing mission over Syrian positions in Lebanon. His pilot/friend, Mark T. Lange was killed when their AE-6 Intruder was hit by a Soviet-made heat-seeking missile. Goodman ejected, sustaining only some superficial injuries. The Syrian government had declared Goodman would be released only upon the U.S. Marines pull-out from Beirut. Now, five days after the Country Preacher, Jesse Jackson, had set foot on Syrian soil, the decision had been made to release Goodman to Reverend Jackson and the U.S. authorities.

At the precise instant that the interpreter finished that brief statement of the Foreign Secretary, Jesse shot up from his chair as if a hot poker had been put to his posterior. For a split-second, he seemed transfixed in disbelief. Then he grabbed Khaddam and in Oriental fashion, kissed him on both cheeks. He recovered his composure and quickly called for a prayer of thanksgiving. Fervently, in traditional but diplomatic tone, he thanked God for helping to ''break the cycle of pain.'' In irreverent fashion, I peeked at our circle of prayer and I saw the Foreign Minister's eyes glisten with tears. I was crying too.

The prayer circle.

At 11:30 a.m., Damascus time, just a little more than an hour later, Lt. Robert Goodman would be a free man. After the first euphoria of Khaddam's announcement had passed, there remained the practical steps necessary to effect Goodman's release. The Secretary informed us that because Goodman was military personnel, the U.S. government had to be involved. The U.S. ambassador, Robert Paganelli, had been summoned and was waiting in an antechamber. On our way out of Khaddam's office, Paganelli and a couple of his staffers were on their way in. I had hurriedly alerted Jackson that we had to insure our position of strength in case of any embassy "hanky panky" e.g. the spiriting away of Goodman after his release. I suppose the reader will be sympathetic to my organizational paranoia. In any event, as we passed each other, I approached our ambassador and said firmly, *Mr. Ambassador, Reverend Jackson would like to speak to you just as soon as you're finished with Mr. Khaddam.*

With Hadad's help, a private room nearby was set aside for this purpose. Before we could exchange any reactions to this fantastic turn of events, Paganelli was at the door. Any Syrian personnel was politely excused and the door closed for privacy. I spoke first:

Preparing for "woodshed" meeting.

Mr. Ambassador, Paganelli did not seem comfortable to me; *we wanted to be sure that there would be no problem surrounding Reverend Jackson personally escorting Lt. Goodman back to the States.*

Paganelli's response was testy. *Lt. Goodman is being released to Mr. Jackson AND the U.S. Ambassador.*

Silent until now, Jackson broke in, *But Khaddam saw me first!*

This was no time for a war of words. I'd just go ahead and "bell the cat" and get the matter settled. *Mr. Paganelli, we have some real concern that Lt. Goodman will not be available to those of us who worked so hard to have him released.*

Paganelli's back straightened up abruptly; the corners of his mouth tightened. Through clenched teeth, he almost hissed his answer. *We have no intention whatsoever of making Lt. Goodman unavailable to you or anyone else!*

I slapped my knee, down-home style and gave a hollow laugh and replied, *Fine, just wanted to make sure we had some understanding.*

The whirlwind of the next few moments moved so swiftly that my recollection of sequence is probably a little muddled. I do know that Jesse Jackson gave me two assignments right after Paganelli's departure from our "woodshed" meeting. The first was to round up the rest of the delegation and assemble them at the U.S. Embassy, just around the corner. The Syrians were processing the papers that Paganelli had signed and making the physical arrangements to bring Goodman to the Foreign Ministry. The estimate was that the announcement of Goodman's release could be made at 11:30 here at the Foreign Ministry with Jackson, Khaddam and Paganelli present.

Florence Tate and I grabbed my car and returned to the Sheraton where I instructed her to pass the word to all mission members and meet me at the embassy. I raced back to the Foreign Ministry. No word had yet come on Goodman's status. I walked through the narrow street adjoining the Foreign Ministry to our embassy. Everyone was present. Florence told me she had spread the word that a major news briefing would be held at the hotel at 12:30. It is at this point that my recollection is most muddled.

I do recollect that I suggested turning all the cars around in the courtyard of the embassy in case we had to move swiftly. I anticipated that might save a few minutes. For some reason, I entered the embassy itself and went upstairs and was introduced to several members of the embassy clerical staff. I must confess that I was on "cloud 9" with the news of Goodman's imminent release. My impression is that Mr. Jackson was on the premises also because I recall the presence of the Secret Service. If not, why else would they have been there? In any event, the moment arrived for us to proceed to the Foreign Ministry. It took only a few moments. It was in the moments just prior to Goodman's actual release that I received my second assignment from Jackson.

The second assignment the Country Preacher laid on me was responsibility for arranging the "Victory" luncheon. Somewhere between gathering the mission members and the actual release of Goodman, it occurred to the Country Preacher that a meal of fellowship would be appropriate. I was instructed to include everyone; our delegation, the press corps, the Secret Service, Syrian Political Security, the embassy staff – *everyone!*

It must have been close to 11:30 when I located Hamzeh and explained that I needed to call the hotel immediately.

Come with me, please, he said quietly and uncharacteristically, smiling. His office was just down the corridor from the room where we had held the "woodshed" meeting with Paganelli. It was a generous office made smaller by two massive desks butted together, front to front. After he dialed the number for me, I asked for the banquet manager, a Mr. Ghandi of East Indian extraction. I made a quick addition in my head and gave Ghandi confirmed reservations for seventy-five. He asked what menu would we prefer? Chicken, of course.

As the only known historian of this stunning, spectacular and scintillating event of American foreign policy, you can imagine my chagrin to report that by the time the luncheon was arranged, Goodman had been released and the announcement made jointly by Jackson and Paganelli on the front steps of the Foreign Ministry. I had missed the whole thing! To add to my chagrin, everyone had boarded their respective vehicles and were enroute to the Sheraton. They had left *me* (smile).

Disconsolate that I had missed the release after putting all of my skills and experience into this effort, I knew there was still work to do. I'd call the hotel and get someone to send a car for me. I underestimated the reaction to Goodman's release in Damascus.

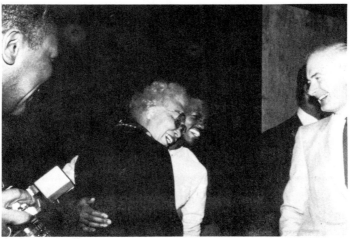

Dr. Adair with Lt. Goodman.

When Hamzeh Hamzeh rang up the Sheraton again, there was no answer for twenty minutes. I learned later that upon the arrival of Jackson and Goodman at the hotel, the jubilation was so great that all hotel services were interrupted for about twenty minutes. The Syrian public was as ecstatic as we were.

By the time I returned to the hotel, the press briefing for Lieutenant Goodman was in full sway. Jackson in command as always, was gracious enough to invite Paganelli to participate. The U.S. Ambassador was not nearly so gracious to Mr. Jackson. Despite relentless badgering fromt he press, he would not budge from his "party line" response to questions about Mr. Jackson's role in freeing Goodman. He would only concede that "many hands" had made Goodman's release possible.

Lt. Goodman was the epitome of naval spit and polish, reserved and correct to a fault. He was grateful for Mr. Jackson's efforts but not profuse. He said nothing that would in anyway reflect on his branch of service or the United States government. He was anxious to see his family and hoped he could return to his squadron as soon as possible.

It must be said that Jesse Louis Jackson was not fatuous in the moment of his greatest personal and career success. He repeatedly gave the "glory to God" for this instance of "breaking the cycle of pain." It was he who insisted on a photograph of all the mission members flanking Goodman with hands clasped, American sports-style. If ever there was a moment for a public figure to swagger, this was it. Jesse Jackson did not swagger. The press conference closed with Jackson presiding over the ceremony of removing the blue ribbons we had been wearing since the Sunday after the Memphis meeting.

The "Victory" Handclasp
Robert Paganelli, Lt. Goodman, Jackson and the author.

The "Victory" luncheon was the closest thing to
revelry during our stay in Syria. It was a heart-
warming sight to see the intermingling of cultures
and interest that turned on the release of this young
Black naval lieutenant. Colonel Hisam and Patrick
Miller, the Secret Service and the Syrian Political
Security; Jesse Jackson and the American media,
often protagonists; Christians and Muslims, Protestants and Catholics, Presbyterians and Baptists,
Black and white; a celebration over baked chicken!

Once we returned to 367, some other concerns
came to fore. There was a call for Goodman from

Mission members with friends. (l-r standing) Howard, Porter, Theobald, Farrakhan, Thomas, Jackson, Col. Hisam, Interpreter, Jesse, Jr., Adair, Ambassador, Paganelli; (kneeling) Jonathan Jackson, Walker, Muhammad.

Ronald Reagan and Goodman's calls to his family. Eugene Wheeler had issued the order for all luggage to be checked to be placed in the corridor by four o'clock. Pat O'Brien of the embassy staff was getting a C-141 out of Rhein-Mainz, Germany, re-fitted for the first leg of our return trip to the States. Somehow in the midst of all that was happening, Jesse Louis Jackson had managed to extract permission from the Syrian government for a military transport plane to land on Syrian soil. When I was a child, on summer evenings, we often played Hide-and-Seek. The signal to start was "Ready? Set? Go!" It was "Ready, Set, Go" time in Damascus.

The networks were dying to get Goodman on camera for the morning shows on the East coast. Naturally he was apprehensive about going on camera in his prison garb. Jesse Jr. was given the task by his father to round up the suitable wardrobe for this appearance, a shirt from here, a tie from there, slacks here, etc. At some point, the jacket provided didn't quite have the fit Goodman preferred. Jesse Jr. asked me for one of my blazers (actually one was the jacket to my black suit but the white buttons gave a blazer effect). I was bemused when the commentator mentioned Goodman's appearance in a "finely tailored suit." It was that jacket with the white buttons! A piece of my clothing had gone down in history.

There's one vignette of the aftermath of Goodman's release that warrants telling here. At some point of our celebration of Goodman's release, we were all gathered in Jackson's suite following the luncheon, Ed Theobald and I were standing next to each other. The Leader had just led us in a prayer of thanksgiving, keeping our focus that it was the Lord's work, not ours.

Isn't this great! Theobald said. *I just can't believe it!*

It's fantastic, that's what it is, I said.

Both of our cups were running over. We grabbed each other and gave each other a warm bear-hug. How incongrous, I thought. A white Catholic from New Hampshire and a Black Baptist from Harlem hugging each other in Damascus, Syria.

Eugene Wheeler, a businessman from Los Angeles, who put his enterprises on hold to assist with Jackson's presidential bid, pulled me aside and said, *Wyatt, we ought to get Goodman some clothes. He shouldn't have to wear those clothes home.*

I agreed. Wheeler is ordinarily the Keeper of the Exchecquer for the Jackson party but his cash flow had been hard hit by cashing checks for our mission members. I volunteered my assistance (since I was a banker) with the additional commitment that Freedom Bank would pay for Goodman's first suit and Canaan Church, his topcoat. The other minor items would be

Goodman inspects new clothes as Wheeler looks on.

no problem. Within an hour, Wheeler personally made two trips to the Souk to see that Goodman was satisfactorily outfitted for the journey home.

It was almost dark as we climbed into our "assigned cars" for the last time. Just as we were leaving Mr. Jackson's suite, two unexpected visitors came by to pay their respects; Colonel Hisam of Syria's Political Security and the interpreter who had translated for Mr. Jackson in every instance. The Country Preacher was deeply touched. As we sped to the tarmac of the Damascus Aerodrome, it was all of these little things like the visit of these two gentlemen that made me feel a little sad in leaving.

Too soon, it seems, we were gathered in that same room we occupied upon our arrival. The media people were "still taking care of business," asking questions of any and everyone, electronic flashes blinked relentlessly. I was the last to enter the room while the press

Friends stop to pay respects.

Dr. Thomas and driver.

positioned themselves to record our departure from Syria.

Jackson was presiding over the departure "ceremony."

We need to thank God for all that has happened here and for the new friends we've made. Paganelli and his staff complement were in place. Khaddam's deputy foreign minister was present again as was my new friend, Khalil Abu Hadad, and of course the ever-present Secret Service. *I want to ask Louis to give a prayer and Wyatt Walker with his disgusting, organized self, to dismiss us with a benediction.*

I knew that the Reverend Jesse Louis Jackson had just paid me a great compliment.

Within a few moments of these prayers and farewells, our C-141 roared down the tarmac and into the black sky over this ancient city of the Mid-East. Good-bye, Damascus!

Home Again So Soon

If you've never been on a C-141 military transport, you've missed one of the great experiences of modern air travel. Luxury, it is not; spartan is a more apt description. Our luggage was piled helter-skelter in what would be the middle aisle of a commercial jet, then secured with wide, nylon straps. Our seating was along the fuselage sides of the plane, almost hammock style. The roar of those four mighty engines reverberated throughout the aircraft. We had to literally, shout to each other in normal conversation. First it was hot, then it was cold. Most important of all, we were on our way home!

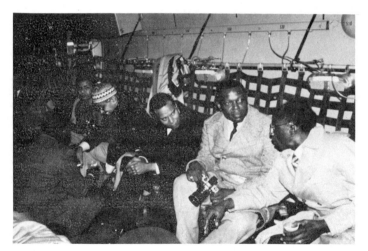

Aboard C-141. (l-r) Tate, Walker, Farrakhan, Muhammad and Thomas.

Our lift-off was just about seven p.m. Damascus time. We all presumed that within four hours or so we'd be touching down at the U.S. military installation at Rhein-Mainz near Frankfurt. We presumed wrong. In the excitement accompanying Goodman's release, I had missed the intelligence that because this was a military aircraft, it was prohibited from flying over several European nations in our normal flight path. After four hours of bumpy flying, we learned that our route to Frankfurt was due west across the Mediterranean to Sicily, thence north into Europe and on to Rhein-Mainz. The normal 3½ hours flight took nearly eight hours over this circuitous path.

During this long flight, it should be reported that the chap from Reuters did 'seek me out' and offered his apologies for his uncouth behavior. I accepted them and *thank you Akbar Muhammad* (smile).

The Press. (l-r) Jack White, Time Magazine, Anna Clopet, Newsweek, Julia Jones, Jackson Campaign, D. Michael Cheers, Johnson Publications.

At Rhein-Mainz touchdown, the Secret Service informed me that Goodman would deplane and proceed directly onto Air Force 2 which would be parked parallel to our docking spot. My paranoia came to the fore again. While I was napping on that long flight, Goodman (so I was informed later) crawled up into the upper reaches of the C-141 and emerged in full dress uniform. I *knew* there was going to be some kind of switch and leave Jesse out in the cold. My fears were groundless.

While Mr. Jackson was being interviewed live on ABC television by Ken Walker (no relation), I hustled over to the Chief of Protocol headquarters about six hundred yards away. We were suddenly out of the environment of a Mediterranean climate. The early morning temperature at Rhein-Mainz with the wind-chill factor, was near zero. Upon gaining entrance, I identified myself to the officer in charge (a bird colonel) who was very gracious and efficient. In a few minutes, a line was reserved for Mr. Jackson's transatlantic call to Senator Charles Percy and Mrs. Jackson. In short order, hot tea and coffee was provided in a private salon for Mr. Jackson's comfort. On board the C-141, Bill Howard, Jesse Jackson and I had determined that there was no need in our rushing out of Rhein-Mainz in order to land at Andrews Air Force Base at 3 or 4 o'clock in the morning. It seemed to us more prudent to take our time, make a couple of "important" calls, have a spot of tea or coffee and arrive at Andrews Air Force base about seven when the morning news shows would be going on the air. That's exactly what we did.

Once aboard Air Force 2, racism reared its ugly head. The fifteen of us, who in my view had risked much in the effort that succeeded in securing Goodman's release, were forced to scramble for sitting space while navy brass, well rested, warmed and fed, were already ensconced in the most comfortable seats aboard. We did express our unhappiness and Mr. Jackson and a couple of others were seated comfortably but eight of us including Dr. Adair, had to ride across the Atlantic in bench seats in the lounge. Our unhappiness was compounded when some duty officer announced we had too many passengers and either someone from the mission or from the press corps would have to get off. After considerable wrangling (the press people flatly refused to budge) Florence Tate volunteered to get off. Absolutely not, we chorused. Let some of this Navy brass catch another plane!

In a few minutes, we were airborne and no one had to deplane.

This was the first time in nearly thirty Atlantic crossing that I had to ride side-saddle. We made the best of it twisting and turning until finally with the first pencil line of dawn behinds us, the Captain announced we would be on the ground at Andrews Air Force Base in a few minutes.

I have had my quarrels with this land of mine but in my heart of hearts, I know that it is the greatest country in the world and I am not ashamed to say that I was glad to be back in the United States of America. Our arrival at the propitious moment of morning news shows has stamped that January 4th morning in America's collective memory. For some reason that I do not yet know, I chose to exit from the rear door of Air Force Two and by-pass the hoopla at the front end. I think it's because I take serious pride in being an "organization man" and at this point my task was finished. Leave the lights and interviews to Jesse and the others.

This was the first time in nearly thirty Atlantic crossing that I had to ride side-saddle. We made the best of it twisting and turning until finally with the first pencil line of dawn behind us, the Captain announced we would be on the ground at Andrews Air Force Base in a few minutes.

across the land. Even with my back-door exit, I soon hear familiar voices calling, *Wyatt! Wyatt Tee!* I turned to see first W. Franklin Richardson, General Secretary of the National Baptist Convention, Curtis Harris, a Virginia pastor and SCLC cell-mate, Eugene Jackson of Unity Broadcasting and Ed Lewis, publisher of Essence Magazine, both directors of Freedom National Bank, Ducky Birts, a childhood chum from Camden, N.J., Earl Graves of Black Enterprise Magazine, Congressman Walter Fauntroy, Emma Chappell, Dr. Milton Reid, publisher of Norfolk Journal and Guide, and Byron Lewis of Uniworld.

The mission members were led into the terminal building while Mr. Jackson and Goodman made brief arrival statements; then herded into limousines for the twenty-five minute ride to Walter Fauntroy's New Bethel Baptist Church for an eight o'clock prayer service. Goodman was spirited away from Andrews to Walter Reed Hospital for an immediate medical examination and a private reunion with his family. They all would surface later in the afternoon for a hastily arranged welcoming reception in the White House Rose Garden.

Prayer service in Washington, D.C. (l-r) Congressman Fauntroy, Mrs. Jackson, Jesse Jackson and author.

The religious service at New Bethel Baptist Church was an old-fashioned down home church meeting of the saints. For me, one of the highlights of that gathering was the spirited, teary-eyed, statement of the Syrian ambassador, Rafic Jouejati. The Reverend Jesse Louis Jackson was of course, the principal speaker and centerpiece of this early morning religious showcase. With great sensitivity, he personally introduced each member of the mission and thanked everyone for their interest and prayers.

My last official act, in concert with the Secret Service, was to physically go to the pulpit and gently move the Country preacher while he was at the peroration of his sermon, in order that a delegation, almost twice the size of that which traveled to Syria, might keep its date with Goodman and Ronald Reagan at the White House. In an exchange of notes before he was presented to speak, the Leader insisted that I join the others for the White House shin-dig. I opted to skip it as mild protest against Reagan. For a President who makes phone calls to Super Bowl winners, I felt keenly that he should have met us at the airport.

I caught the next Eastern shuttle to New York and flung myself into the arms of my waiting wife, Theresa Ann. So soon, it seemed, I was home again!

The White House Rose Garden.

POSTLOGUE: The Fall Out

In the several days that followed our return from Damascus, it began to dawn on me just how "big" the story of Goodman's release really was here in the U.S. My wife had thoughtfully saved the daily papers since our departure and I could not believe the snide tone of the articles and editorials. I had assumed wrongly, that once our mission had actually gone to Syria to seek Goodman's release, the general public and the fourth estate would set aside their public and private prejudices against Jesse Jackson and hope for our eventual success. I was dismayed to read in retrospect a *New York Times* editorial of December 30th at the very time we were entering a war zone in the Mid-East. I was aghast at still another, once we had succeeded in our mission. That editorial stance was mirrored in the Gannett chain under the cynical caption, Opportunism in Damascus.*

It developed that *Newsweek*, William Buckley Jr., George Will and others, all contrived some design to begrudge Jesse Jackson the well-deserved plaudits he earned for his bold and faith-filled inititiative. Ronald Reagan turned out to be the most gracious of all protagonists. A *Time* magazine quote is instructive: "Awakened at 5:30 a.m. with the news, a genuinely ebullient Reagan gave Jackson his full due. 'If that guy could get him out and we couldn't, more power to him.'" The leadership in the Democratic party, in my view, was no more than polite in its assessment.

Within forty-eight hours of our return, the *New York Post*, America's gift to yellow journalism, broke the "big" story as to "who paid the hotel bill" exposing its complete naivete about ground rules and

*See Appendix "H" and "I".

133

dynamics of international diplomacy. Jesse Jackson and party, were guests of President Hafez al-Assad. Once we were on Syrian soil, we were the guests of the Republic of Syria.

The *l'addition*, as the French say, is clear. Lt. Robert O. Goodman is a free man. He would not have been early this year without the courage and faith of Jesse Louis Jackson and his companions. For a brief moment, the temperature in the Mid-east cauldron was lowered and the 1800 Marines did come home.

The benefits to Jesse Jackson were enormous. If he had not been considered a serious candidate before Damascus, he certainly had to be, after Damascus. The relentless media attention in this land waiting for him to fall on his face had no choice but to record his spectacular success. This consequently gave an added if not critical boost to his candidacy for the Democratic nomination. There are few detractors now, in the wake of Jackson's equally spectacular bid for the Presidential nomination. Thrown in along the way, was the odyssey to Cuba and the resultant release of a considerable number of political prisoners there.

Of course, there remain those who gleefully point to the "Hymie" remark and the Farrakhan association as disclaimer's to Jesse Jackson's true greatness. I remind the reader of another beleagured Black hero who weathered all the "slings and arrows" of America's systemic racism, in life and death — Martin Luther King, Jr. It is the mantle of King that has fallen on the shoulders of Jesse Louis Jackson and Damascus was the *Zeitgeist* – the fullness of time. Mind you, it is not because Jesse desired the mantle (and he may have), but it happened because God willed it so. The Damascus adventure represents the chief watershed in the development of an international human rights hero who happens to be Black. The crucial ingredient in the development is that in Jesse as in Martin, God found a spirit who would get into a righteous struggle even when the outcome was uncertain. That is the ultimate lesson of Damascus. It was indeed a *journey of faith.*

APPENDIX

Statement by Reverend Jesse Jackson following State Department Briefing, December 27, 1983

The Middle East is a flashpoint of a hot and cold war. The American troops there have neither the authorization nor the capacity to proceed with an undeclared war without a clear description as to who the enemy is, or what is the foreign policy basis of their mission. This situation confuses the posture of all of our captives in Lebanon – the United States Marines and sends mixed signals to the parties to the peace process there.

The use of Lt. Goodman as war bait or for barter is not ethical. At this point, Lt. Goodman must know that the American people are pulling for him and that he is not going to be a sacrifical lamb on two political fronts; one front involves the motives of the Syrians in holding and keeping him hostage and the other involves those of the U.S. Neither is it our motive to be concerned about Lt. Goodman only because he is Black. Actually, the race issue was created not by us, but by the wide-spread perception and, indeed our relevation, that the Reagan Administration is apparently not doing all that it could to secure Lt. Goodman's release.

In the process of appealing to President Assad for his release, as a gesture of good faith, the Rumsfeld revelation shocked all of us. The idea of a special envoy from the White House, who had met with Syrian officials without raising the Lt. Goodman issue was a demoralizing issue – it embarrassed the White House and now there is a lot of activity around and focused on Lt. Goodman. It now means that the issue of Lt. Goodman's release is now on the *front burner*, and that no future Special Envoys can ignore the Good-man issue.

I have met with President Assad of Syria on a previous occasion. I have known religious leaders there and I have visited Syria. Our moral appeal for the release of Lt. Goodman has meaning, therefore, for both Americans and Syrians. We appeal to President Assad to release Lt. Goodman as a gesture of good faith, as a way of relieving some of the special tensions and to enhance the focus on the peace negotiations and de-emphasize the use of military solutions – which within the context of the Middle East problem have never proven satisfactory. Therefore, in mounting this mission, we do not choose to defy our Government, but to seek to change its priorities – from those of war to those of peace, from the politics of military solutions to the politics of freedom for Lt. Goodman.

Thus, our moral appeal still stands for the United States to adopt a foreign policy in the Middle East based on peace and not on a military solution, and for President Assad for joining the peace process in the Middle East, beginning with the release of Lt. Goodman as a good faith gesture. Our *collective wisdom* must get us to the negotiating table and away from the combat zone, toward peace for all in that region of the world.

Jackson Mission Roster to Syria

The Rev. Jesse Louise Jackson, Leader

Dr. Thelma Adair	Minister Akbar Muhammad
Minister Louis Farrakhan	Dr. Thomas Porter
Dr. M. William Howard	Ms. Florence Tate
Jesse Jackson Jr.	Edward Theobald
Jonathan Jackson	Dr. Andrew Thomas
Ms. Julia Jones	Dr. Wyatt Tee Walker
The Rev. Jack Mendelsohn	Eugene Wheeler

APPENDIX C

```
                    JACKSON MISSION TO SYRIA

                    GENERAL DECORUM **

1.  DAMASCUS IS POPULATED BY NATIONALS OTHER THAN SYRIANS. SECURITY
    WILL BE THE PRIME CONSIDERATION.

2.  ALL CONVERSATIONS WILL BE MONITORED INDOORS. REMEMBER, WE ARE
    GUESTS IN SYRIA

3.  WHATEVER YOUR PERSONAL VIEWS, YOU REPRESENT THE U.S. NONE OF US
    WISH TO EMBARASS OUR COUNTRY OR MR. JACKSON.

4.  AVOID SALADS, UNCOOKED VEGETABLES, DAIRY PRODUCTS, ETC.

5.  DRINK BOTTLED WATER ONLY & CHECK TO SEE THAT SEAL IS UNBROKEN.

6.  ANY USE OF BEVERAGE ALCOHOL SHOULD BE DONE IN THE PRIVACY OF
    YOUR ROOM.

7.  DEPARTURE TIMES MUST BE PROMPT.

8.  ALL CAR ASSIGNMENTS ARE PERMANENT UNTTIL DEPARTURE: NO
    EXCEPTIONS!

9.  COMMUNICATIONS RE:DAILY SCHEDULE WILL BE TRANSMITTED DAILY OR
    OR MORE FREQUENTLY, IF NECESSARY, ROOM BY ROOM.

10.  OTHER NOTES:       CUSTOMS AND TABOOS
                        NEW YEAR'S CELEBRATION
```

A Brief Introduction
To The Syrian Arab Republic*

History

Syria lies in the heart of the Middle east between Mesopotamia and the Nile, an area in which there has been human activity for almost 150,000 years. Syria's rich archaeological heritage gives evidence of the many advanced civilizations which have dominated the country throughout its history.

Early inhabitants of Syria were largely Semitic peoples whose prescence was reinforced by successive waves of invasion by other Semitic proples. As Syria was dominated by one empire after another, the permanent settlers became prosperous traders.

From the 16th Century B.C. until the Fifth Century B.C. Syria, which then included what is present-day Jordan, Lebanon, Syria and Israel, was ruled in succession by Egyptians, Aramaeans, Assyrians and Babylonians. Semitic rule of Syria ended with the coming of the Persians in 500 B.C. The Persians in turn were defeated by Alexander the Great in 333 B.C. After the death of Alexander the Great, his empire was divided among his generals. One of them, Seleucus, received Persia and much of the Near East, including Syria. during the time of Alexander and the Seleucids, Hellenistic culture flourished throughout the Near East.

In 64 B.C. Syria was conquered by the Roman general Pompey and became a Roman province. Roman rule brought with it peace and prosperity for many years. The Romans built among other things, roads, aqueducts and wells that remained in use down to modern times.

When the Roman Empire was divided in half, Syria became part of the Eastern Roman Empire, which had its capital at Constantinople (modern Istanbul).

In 636 A.D., four years after the death of Mohammed, his followers defeated a Byzantine army, and as a result,

*Extract of manual prepared by U.S. Embassy staff, Damascus, Syria.

Syria became a Moslem Arab land. Damascus became the capital of the Omayyad Caliphate, a large Arab empire that eventually stretched from India across Persia, Syria, all of northern Africa to Andalous (Spain). Although the Omayyad period lasted only ninety years, Syria so thoroughly assimilated its culture that eventually Arabic became the dominant language and Islam the dominant religion of the country.

From the breakup of the Omayyad Empire in 750 A.D. until the French mandate in 1920, Syria was a province of successive empires; the Abbassids whose capital was in Baghdad, the Mameluke sultans of Egypt, and the Ottoman Turks. This period of Syrian history also saw invasions by the Christian crusaders from the west and the Mongols from the east.

In the first World War the Turks were defeated by a combined British and Arab army and forced out of Syria. After the war Syria was given to France under a League of Nations mandate. In 1920 Lebanon was separated from Syria. The French introduced many Western ideas and developments into Syria and Lebanon, but Arab nationalism was strong, and the mandate was unpopular.

Although a consititution was drawn up in 1930 which made Syria a republic, it did not become independent until 1941. When the Second World War ended the French attempted to re-establish their control over Syria, but this prompted widespread revolt which resulted in the final evacuation of French forces in 1946.

From 1946 to 1970 the country had a number of different governments, including a three-year union with Egypt under the name of the United Arab Republic. In 1970 the present president, general Hafez al-Assad, head of the military wing of the Baath party, came into power.

Syria today cover 71,500 square miles and has a population of about 9,200,000 people. Damascus is the capital and largest city. Other important cities are Aleppo, Homs, Hama and Lattakia. Arabic is the official language of the country, with English and French the principal foreign languages taught in secondary schools and universities.

Islam

Islam and the Arab world are to most Westerners as exotic as the Arabian Nights – and as baffling as the most recent crises in the Middle East. Beyond these impressions, most Westeners have little knowledge of the world's second largest religion.

Islam is the religion of more than 700 million people occupying one of the wealthiest and most strategic parts of the world, stretching from Indonesia in the Pacific to Morocco on the Atlantic. In Syria almost 90% of the people embrace one form or another of Islam (most are Sunnis, but many are Alawite, Druze, or Ismailis) and approximately 10% are Christians. There is a small Jewish community in Damascus and Aleppo.

In Arabic, Islam means "submission" and in some interpretations refers to "peace, purity and obedience" In the religious sense, Islam is submission to the will of God, and a Muslim is one who believes and practices the concepts of Islam. (Incidentally, the religion preached by the Prophet Mohammed has been called by some outsiders "Mohammedanism" and its followers "Mohammedans", but these are misnomers based on the misconception that Muslims worship Mohammed – and the term is offensive to Muslims.)

In the traditional sense, Islam is not a new religion but a belief taught to mankind by a series of prophets, each revealing a book – the Torah brought by Moses, Psalms by David, and the Gospel by Jesus. Mohammed was the last of the prophets, bringing the book of the Koran, which completes and supersedes all previous revelations. More commonly, the term Islam is restricted to the final phase of the sequence of revelations, that of Mohammed and the Koran.

Mohammed was born in 570 A.D. in Mecca in Arabia of a noble family. While a merchant at the age of forty, he experienced his first revelatin from the angel Gabriel during solitary meditation. He was compelled to preach a new revelation, gathered followers, and finally, due to incresing hostility and persecution, was forced to flee to Medina with his closest converts in 622 A.D. This migration, *Hegira* begins the year One of the Muslim calendar.

For eight years Mohammed presided over the Muslim community, instructing them in the Islamic faith through revelations. In 630 A.D. Mohammed returned to Mecca, which became Islam's most holy city, and its Kaaba, the most holy shrine.

In 632 A.D. Mohammed died at the age of 63 after a brief illness and was buried in Medina. He was succeeded as leader by four *Caliphs*. The succession of the fifth caliph resulted in a division of sects – the followers of Ali, the fourth caliph (*Shiat Ali*) became *Shiites*, and the followers of Muawiyah, the governor of Syria who declared himself the fifth Caliph (who never recognized Ali) and founded the Omayyad Caliphate, became *Sunnis*. Sunnis (those who follow the *Sunna*, the ways of the Prophet) became the largest religious group in Syria.

Islam requires faith in the unity of God, angels and apostles of God, Books of God, the Day of Judgment – man's accountability for his deeds, and life after death. Islam provides definitie guidelines for all men to follow. It gives a comprehensive code of life, dealing with its social, economic, moral, and spiritual aspects. Islam defines a system of duties, the fulfillment of which enables a believer to live a righteous life in this world and to prepare himself for the next.

There are five basic practices of Islam, the "Five Pillars of Worship":

1. **Shahada** Testimony, declaration of faith that there is no God but God (Allah) and that Mohammed is his prophert.

2. **Salat** Ritual prayer offered five times daily – at sunrise, mid-day, afternoon, sunset, and evening, facing Mecca. Times of prayer are

indicated by the call to prayer from the minaret of a mosque.

3. **Zakat**   An annual voluntary charity tax of 2½% of wealth, exempting necessities such as house and clothing.

4. **Sawm**   Fasting: abstention from food, drink and sexual relations between the hours of sunrise and sunset, during the month of *Ramadan* (ninth month of the Muslim year, the month the Koran was "sent down"). The purpose is purification of the soul.

5. **Hajj**   Pilgrimage to Mecca once in a lifetime, provided one has the means, during the 7th-10th days of the 12th month of the Muslim year.

The Muslim year has two canonical festivals: **Id al Adha** – Festival of Sacrifices or Greater Festival following Hajj, commemorating Prophet Abraham's willingness to sacrifice his son; and **Id al Fitr** – Festival of Breaking Fast or Lesser Festival celebrating the end of Ramadan.

Jackson Mission to Syria

31 December
RELIGIOUS LEADERS CONVOCATION
Ministry of Religion & Endowment Headquarters

ATTENDANCE

Christians

Bishop Abu Mukh	Greek Catholic rep of the Patriarch
Patriarch Zakka I	Head of the Syrian Orthodox Church in the World
Patriarch Agnatius IV Hazim	Head of Greek Orthodox Church of the Orient
Bishop Samaha	Greek Orthodox Community in South Syria (Golan Heights)
Bishop Kolpakian	Armenian Orthodox Church, Syria & Greece
The Rev. Adeeb Awad	Head of the Protestant Community in Syria (United Presbyterian)

Moslems

Dr. Ibrahim Salgini	Dean of the College of Islamics & Jurisdiction
Dr. Muhammad A.L. Earfour	Teacher in College of Islamics
Dr. Wahdi Zuhaih	Teacher, College of Islamics
Sheik Shawkei Ali Gibah	Teacher, College of Islamics
Sheik Muhammad A.F. Khatbib	Teacher, College of Islamics
Sheik Ziad Eddin Ayubi	Teacher, College of Islamics
Sheik Abdullah al Sayyed	Teacher, College of Islamics

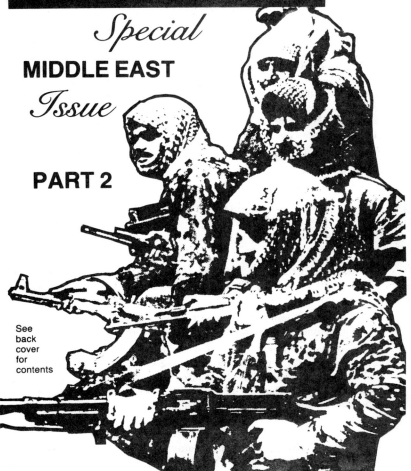

Freedomways

A QUARTERLY REVIEW OF THE FREEDOM MOVEMENT

Volume 23
Number 3
1983
$2.00

Special

MIDDLE EAST

Issue

PART 2

See
back
cover
for
contents

Liberation Theology and the Middle East Conflict

by WYATT TEE WALKER

THE AUTHENTIC theology of the New Testament is a theology of liberation—personal, political, economic, social. My slave ancestors knew Jesus as the Liberator of body and spirit, in this world and in the next. However, one must recognize that the phrase "Liberation Theology" has a new currency in the context of the late 20th century, in light of the struggles for freedom which have all but destroyed colonialism in the world. My remarks here will reflect my allegiance to both the old and the new content of this concept.

The stakes in the Middle East are enormously high and complex. Armed conflict between Arab and Jew has had little respite since the end of World War I. We are on the brink of yet another war in that region as this article goes to press. In the midst of the present saber-rattling taking place in the Bekaa Valley and throughout southern Lebanon, some constants prevail:

- Israel insists, rightly, on recognition and secure borders.
- The Palestinians demand, rightly, a geographical homeland with full sovereignty.
- The United States is working feverishly to maintain its influence in this sensitive region of the world.
- The Soviet Union is doing the same.
- The Arab nations unanimously subscribe to the concept of a Palestinian state but are disunited on the strategy for attaining that goal, as evidenced by the divergent perspectives of Egypt, Saudi Arabia and Syria.
- The rest of the world waits with bated breath, fearful that a spark might make the horror of nuclear war a reality.

Amid these concerns, some of them narrow and others necessarily broad, seldom is the issue of rightness raised. What moral and theological issues are at stake? Does the cause of the Palestinians fit the profile of a liberation movement? Is their struggle grounded in a theology of liberation (Islam may well have a liberation theology as does Christianity)?

Wyatt Tee Walker, formerly chief aide to Martin Luther King, Jr., is the Senior Minister of Harlem's Canaan Baptist Church of Christ. An essayist and the author of three books, Dr. Walker is active in the world peace movement and has visited the Middle East many times.

Historically, Israel, that sliver of real estate at the eastern end of the Mediterranean, has been the cradle of three world religions—Judaism, Christianity and Islam. Yet, ironically, in the protracted turmoil, little has been said about what is right, moral, and just. It is an understatement to say that there are grave theological implications that bear on the continuing crisis in the Middle East. Despite the strident voices of neo-Zionism in the U.S. and in Israel, some very profound and far-reaching theological questions must be raised and their answers pursued with vigor and tenacity.

The history of the region is as complicated as the issues which confound the search for peace. The Bible tells us that the area now defined as the modern State of Israel was once inhabited by the ancestors of today's far-flung Jewish people. For more than 400 years, they languished in slavery under the pharaohs of Africa. Led by Moses and Joshua, they threw off the yoke of their oppression and reclaimed the area by force from an agricultural people known as Canaanites. The Biblical stance clearly posits this as the land "promised" by God to the house of Israel.

One theological point at issue is, at what juncture in the history of a region shall it be decided who has first claim on the land? Extra-Biblical evidence exists that another people occupied this land prior to the advent of those eponymous heroes, Abraham, Isaac and Jacob. Moreover, because Judaism, Christianity and Islam all developed in the region and its immediate environs under consideration, the question of which adherents have first claim has been in much dispute since the occupation by the legions of Rome.

Nearer to our own time, the Ottoman Turks conquered and held title to the land for several hundred years. Their occupation was ended by World War I and occupation by the British commenced. Further complications ensued from the Balfour Declaration and the British mandate that succeeded it. Thornier still was the infamous, United Nations-sanctioned partition scheme that ultimately brought into being a State of Israel but no State of Palestine, which has resulted in a series of events that fly directly in the face of the United Nations charter itself. The political debacle known as Trans-Jordan provided a woefully unsatisfactory solution that, in any case, was terminated with the Six Day War of 1967. In the course of the aforementioned happenings, countless clashes have occurred between Arab and Jew in what might be charitably called a blood feud. And it appears that after two generations of sporadic, violent warfare, we are no closer to a solution today than we were before World War I.

The Canaanites, prior to Joshua's arrival, could, indeed, make a strong claim to the land in question. But given the facts of history, on what grounds, other than Zionist precepts, can Israel claim *exclusive* right to the territory? Too many different peoples have inhabited this land for any to claim an exclusive right, whether Arab or Jew.

To return to an earlier thought for a moment, it can be said that the land is, in a sense, the land of Moses, the land of Jesus *and* the land of · Mohammed. Thus, on what moral or theological grounds can it—or should it be determined, that a certain posterity has exclusive political or territorial rights?

The facts are these: *Israel exists*. It exists as a political entity with an alleged democratic government and systems of defense (the F-16s are on their way); it is a society possessing industry (diamonds, agriculture, tourism), a cultural tradition, homes, shops. . . people. Israel is formally recognized by the United Nations and by more than 100 nations with whom it exchanges ambassadors. The nation has enjoyed more than a generation of (stormy) existence. At this point, it would be neither moral nor practical for the State of Israel to be dismantled, nor should the notion be contemplated. I hasten to say that I am speaking here of *Israel prior to the 1967 War*. With the return of the West Bank to the Palestinians, it would follow that Israel is entitled to "safe and secure borders." Ironically, since 1967, Israel's neo-Zionist expansionism has rendered all of its borders less safe and less secure. The bid for civil relations between Egypt and Israel made by the late Anwar el-Sadat represented the single exception to clear and present danger at every Israeli border.

Simple truths are sometimes the most profound. As a child, I learned that "two wrongs don't make a right." The venomous hatred and distrust prevailing between the Palestinians and Israelis were predictable if one scrutinizes the history of the region formerly known as Palestine. The influx of European Jews began as early as 1881. The Palestinian people, both Arab and Jew, began involuntarily to make room for these new immigrants. After World War I, the influx proceeded in earnest, with the first rounds of violent conflict commencing over *territory*. By the end of World War II, Jewish immigration had erased nearly 400 Palestinian villages from the face of the earth and expropriated the land on which they stood with the sanction of colonialist Great Britain. Since the creation of the State of Israel in 1948, the expropriation of deeded Arab land has continued apace. Palestinian leaders are very nearly correct when they complain that 96 percent of all the land that constitutes the State of Israel was once "deeded Arab land," precious little of which was bought at a fair price or bought at all. Since the Six Day War, land expropriation on the West Bank has been criminal. And measured against the principles embodied in the United Nations Charter, Israeli conduct generally in the occupied territories makes Israel an international outlaw.

In retrospect, then, the establishment of Israel was at least an error, and more likely a crime. The British violated all morality by giving to the Jewish emigrés that which was not theirs to give. Only a colonialist mentality was capable of imposing this wrong on the people of Palestine. The controlled media in the West, naive about the actual history of how Israel came into being, indict the Palestinians as "terrorists" without regard for the age-old truth that violent conquest begets violence. If one were a Palestinian and could trace one's roots in the land of Palestine for more than 400 years, would not one feel morally bound to reclaim the territory that was taken by force from one's people? Therein lies the prime ingredient of the strife which has convulsed the region, and which has been exacerbated by Israel's increasingly militaristic and violent response.

It has grieved my spirit that no Jewish religious figure of real stature has faced up to and publicly acknowledged the factual, historical account of how Israel was created. I dare any rabbi to read David Manchester's thoroughly documented work, *The Gun and the Olive Branch* and come away from it unaffected. No moral spirit could remain unmoved by this English journalist's dispassionate account of Israel's birth.

On the basis of the historical record, the Palestinians have a territorial claim, the legitimacy of which is unarguable. And it is intriguing that, unlike Israel, the Palestinians do not define their claim as exclusive. Yasir Arafat has clearly stated that upon the establishment of a Palestinian state, all Jewish inhabitants presently there may remain. The Israelis, however, deny Palestinians the right to return to their homes, allow no immigration that is non-Jewish, and restrict the rights of non-Jewish Israeli citizens. (No wonder Zionism draws the charge that it is racist.) The Israeli government is hard-pressed to solve the dilemma at Dimona, where two growing settlements of "Black Hebrews" from the U.S. (by way of Liberia) are ensconced. Their presence is clearly in violation of Israeli immigration policy, but the government's preoccupation with "graver concerns" and its reluctance to deport Blacks from "democratic" Israel have fostered a program of only mild harassment and surveillance.

The Palestinians insist, and they are correct, that they have the right to return to their homeland, which was seized from them illegally. Nearly two million Palestinians have been displaced since Israel's "War of Independence" in 1948. An entire generation of people has lived as refugees, many within the borders of their original homeland. It is simplistic and cruel to insist, as some Zionist supporters do, that the surrounding Arab nations should provide sanctuaries for these refugees. These people are not Jordanians or Lebanese or Syrians or Libyans or Egyptians or Iraqis: They are Palestinians, and Palestine is their home.

The Palestinians have determined that the Palestine Liberation Organization (PLO), a coalition of groups ranging from moderate to zealous, should be their voice to the world. No matter how much this sticks in the Western craw, the Palestinians have made their choice!

Only the aggrieved victims have the right to choose who shall speak for them—that is a fundamental moral and theological issue. At the same time, reality demands that the PLO rethink its hard-line rhetoric about the destruction of Israel. Israel is here to stay. An inflexible stance toward that nation, as part of the theater of revolution, may have some value in maintaining morale, but it is counter-productive in this moment of history when so much is at stake.

As for the military tactics of the PLO: The history of the rape of their people's land dictates the singular objective of reestablishing a Palestinian homeland *by any means necessary!* What other approach is possible against the armed might of the neo-Zionists? Notwithstanding the relentless expansionism of the Begin government, reflected in the building of new Jewish settlements on confiscated Arab land, the labeling of the West Bank, *Judea* and *Samaria*, and the moving of Israel's capital from Tel Aviv to Jerusalem, all of which actions are clearly counterproductive to the pursuit of a true peace in the Middle East—notwithstanding these actions, *the righteousness of the Palestinian cause will not go away.*

The morality and immorality of the conflicts in the Middle East are not altogether the burden of Jew and Arab. The United States must examine the morality (that is, the rightness) of our inordinate military aid to Israel, U.S. military aid to Israel which exceeds foreign military aid to all other nations combined. If the stance of Israel towards a Palestinian state is immoral, and I believe it is, then the U.S. is Israel's partner in crime. We profess ourselves to be a "Christian nation," and our anthem extols our virtue as "the land of the free and the home of the brave." How then, in light of the historical record, can we justify our carte blanche allegiance to Israel, no matter what? Not that I propose cutting off all aid to Israel; that would be an unrealistic proposition. The U.S. perceives Israel as her agent state in the Middle East, and so long as East-West tensions persist, we will not pull out. Moreover, should we pull out, the economy of Israel would collapse. It is bad enough to parent an illegitimate child but worse to withdraw support essential to its survival. What *is* possible and realistic is a more even-handed policy toward the aggrieved community—the Arabs. The United States and Israel must recognize that Israel's future is with her Arab neighbors, and that the Palestinian question must be resolved if there is to be peace in the Middle East. (I cannot resist the conjecture that the so-called Israeli agreement to quit Lebanon is a ploy to free up the F-16s. So much for the morality of the U.S.)

A final consideration regarding the Palestinian cause: Does its profile match those of other struggles whose raison d'être is grounded in liberation theology? The Vietnamese persisted in their liberation struggle for more than 30 years. They resisted the French, the Dutch, the puppets of imperialism, the trickery of the Geneva Accords and, finally, the arrogance of the United States. They achieved their independence, and however imperfect it may be, it is undergirded by their legitimate claim to the land, and by the will of the majority of the Vietnamese people.

Zimbabwe is an even more recent exemplar of the genre. When the racist Rhodesian government held full sway, both Mugabe and Nkomo were labeled "terrorists." But in the broad daylight of that new republic's independence, it has been clear that the real terrorists were Ian Smith and his cohorts, while Mugabe and Nkomo have been revealed as freedom fighters.

Namibia and South Africa are now locked in the paroxysms of liberation. Namibia is near its goal, with the winds of freedom boding ill for the Pretoria government. Both freedom movements have a legitimate, indigenous claim to the land, and they are exercising the will of the majority of their peoples. To the South African government, which exploits their people, Sam Nujoma and Oliver Tambo are terrorists. But the truth of history makes them freedom fighters.

El Salvador, too, leans toward the profile. The U.S. persists in supporting that nation's corrupt, right-wing government against the will of the majority of the Salvadoran people. Indeed, the guerrilla forces could not last without the support of the people in the countryside. Only time will tell, but my guess is that another liberation struggle has been born in the midst of U.S. foreign policy fumbling.

All things considered, the Palestinian cause fits the profile of a struggle for liberation. The Palestinians have a legitimate claim to the land, and the PLO embodies the will of the majority of the people. Further, the prior claim that the Palestinians hold to the land of Palestine entitles them to self-determination and political sovereignty. One could say that the long, violent struggle in the Middle East has become a holy cause fueled by a fervor that borders on fanaticism. But should not all moral persons be fanatics for freedom, justice and equality?

However dismaying to contemplate the truth may be for the Begin government, U.S. Zionists or the muddled minds at Foggy Bottom, the righteous cause of the Palestinian people will not cease and desist. Until a just peace comes to the Middle East, *a luta continua.*

Opportunism in Damascus

YONKER'S HERALD STATESMAN
Tuesday, January 3, 1984

THE RELEASE of Lt. Robert O. Goodman Jr. shows what can happen when an improbable couple like the Rev. Jesse Jackson, Democratic presidential aspirant, and Syria's President Hafez Assad find common ground: a desire to confound and embarrass the Reagan administration.

After all, it was an unpromising venture at the outset. The administration had pointedly warned Jackson that his do-it-yourself diplomacy might only make matters worse. And Syrian officials had repeatedly said that the American Airman held prisoner would be released only when the "war" between Syria and the United States was over.

Our views

But the chemistry of opportunism, particularly on Assad's side, changed all that. Here was a chance for Assad to touch up his own image and to let Jackson — a Reagan political opponent, a critic of the U.S. military involvement in Lebanon and an American conciliatory towards Arabs — make some hay as co-beneficiary, with Lt. Goodman, of an uncharacteristic "humanitarian" gesture by Syria.

You could call the whole episode cynical and theatrical and not be far wrong, but the thing is that it worked. Carrying the implication that the administration's diplomacy has been inadequate or inept, Jackson's coup — when added to the Pentagon report and mounting unrest in Congress — is bound to put President Reagan more than ever on the defensive in trying to justify the Marines' nebulous, high-risk mission.

Which no doubt is exactly what Jackson and Assad had in mind.

Letter to the Editor
Yonker's Hearld Statesman

I cannot tell you the great distress that came over me when I read your editorial of Tuesday, January 3, 1984, "Opportunism in Damascus."

First of all, in light of the almost unanimous agreement that the release of Lt. Robert O. Goodman was a stunning and spectacular success in international relations, your editorial is the epitome of gracelessness. Even Mr. Reagan, whom you allege would be embarassed by Mr. Jackson's efforts was statesman enough to say "You can't quarrel with success . . ." At the White House, of all places, he thanked Mr. Jackson for a job well done and indicated publicly that this might be an "an opportune moment" to explore the possibility of some dialogue between him and Mr. Assad.

You did not mention in your implicit criticism of Mr. Jackson's long-held position that our Marines need to get out of Lebanon, that he has been joined in that view by Mr. Mondale, three former CIA Directors, Schlesinger, Colby and Turner, Tip O'Neil, Speaker of the House and of all people, Republican Senator Charles Percy, Chairman of the Senate Foreign Relations Committee.

Your narrow provincialism shows when you cite Mr. Jackson's stance toward the Arab world as enigmatic. You would avoid your patently obvious yellow journalism by scrutinizing the geo-political realities. Every presidential candidate in memory feels it obligatory to visit Europe and Israel. No presidential candidate feels it obligatory to visit the Arab world, Africa or the Caribbean. It is in America's self-interest that we develop a more even-handed policy toward these other regions especially the Arabs since 47% of energy sources come from the nations that surround the Gulf of Hormuz.

Finally, you call the whole episode "cynical and theatrical." That's half right. Theatrical, yes. The whole world is a stage, viz, President Reagan accepting the blame for the Marine deaths in Beirut. Cynical? Hardly. The stated purpose of our mission was narrow. On humanitarian grounds we would make a moral appeal to the Syrian authorities (Mr. Assad) to release Lt. Robert O. Goodman with the hope that this gesture might alter the military posture of the U.S. and Syria. In the last few days it is apparent that that is happening.

The fundamental problem is that you expected and hoped Mr. Jackson would fail. Your racist mentality cannot digest this stunning and spectacular foreign policy incident that was orchestrated principally by Black religious leaders whom you hold in utter contempt. May I suggest what you do with your editorial: cast it in stone and send it as a gift to Lt. Goodman and his family in Oceana, Virginia.

Wyatt Tee Walker
Chief of Protocol
Jackson Mission to Syria

Canaan Baptist Church of Christ

132 WEST 116TH STREET, NEW YORK, N. Y. 10026 • TELEPHONE 212-866-0301
24 Hour Service

WYATT TEE WALKER, *D.Min., Minister*

January 19, 1984

Letter to the Editors
THE NEW YORK TIMES
229 West 43rd Street
New York, N.Y. 10036

Dear Sirs:

I sincerely hope that there is no deadline on responses to your editorials. I ask you indulgence since I have recently returned from a war zone in the Mid-East and it has taken me a little while to catch up on the news and assume my normal responsibility as a Harlem pastor and responsible citizen. Your editorials of December 30th, 1983 and January 4th, 1984, were insulting and repugnant to me and many Black Americans.

You publish under the exaggerated banner "All The News Fit to Print" and your editorials in this instance are just the opposite. How dare you call Mr. Jackson a carpetbagger! This was not his first meeting with Mr. Assad nor his first visit to the Arab Worl where he is held in considerable esteem. It is a fact that he has met with more Heads of State in the Third World than any other candidate save Walter Mondale. Your editorials wreaks of yellow journalism and torturous logic. Is it "superfluous" and "contemptible" that Lt. Goodman is no longer a prisoner of war? Or that Mr. Reagan had more grace than you to thank Mr. Jackson and send a note to Mr. Assad suggesting they talk instead of fight? You intimate you had inside information that Black Americans were not unhappy with Lt. Goodman's plight being on the back burner. With whom did you check? Summarily, you dismiss the Jackson Mission to Syria as a "shallow venture" and simultaneously impugn Mr. Jackson's integrity. It makes one wonder if the first eight names at the top of your masthead have anything (or everything) to do with your editorial stance re: Jesse Jackson.

The editorial of January 4th added injury to insult. President Reagan, Jesse Jackson's political adversary was genuinely statesmanlike; all the Democratic hopefuls gave Mr. Jackson high marks for his performance. The nation applauded and most of the critics of the mission "ate crow". But *The New York Times* chose to stand with George Will, William F. Buckley and the Gannett Chain. Your deep prejudice shows: Just beneath your snide editorial on Mr. Jackson's Mission to Syria, you place a glowing commentary on Bobby Wagner's distinguished career when everyone except *The New York Times* knows he is a good public servant of modest ability with a famous name.

> Wyatt Tee Walker
> Chief of Protocol
> Jackson Mission to Syria

APPENDIX JJ

DEMOCRATIC
NATIONAL COMMITTEE   *1625 Massachusetts Ave., N.W.   Washington, D.C. 20036   (202) 797-5900*

Charles T. Manatt
Chairman

January 23, 1984

Dr. Wyatt Tee Walker
Chairman of the Board
Freedom National Bank of New York
275 West 125th Street
New York, New York 10027

Dear Dr. Walker:

    Just a note to say how much fun it was seeing you at Reverend Fauntroy's church the other morning. We certainly all are justifiably proud of Reverend Jackson's actions in connection with Lt. Goodwin and I was pleased to be at the prayer meeting for part of the celebration.

    I look forward to seeing you again soon.

> Cordially yours,
>
> Charles T. Manatt
> Chairman

CTM:mm

STATEMENT OF JESSE JACKSON JR.

Reflections On My Damascus Experience

Most of today's leaders seem to be following opinion polls. Fortunately, our Damascus experience demonstrated that the test of true leadership in the midst of crisis, is to mold opinion. Jesus Christ was not very high in the opinion polls of the Roman empire. Nevertheless, it is by His name that history is divided into B.C. and A.D. Even the life of Julius Caesar must be dated by the life of our Saviour!

The mission to Syria was a mission of faith. The Scriptures admonish us that "faith without action" is dead. We might have sat around and waited for Goodman's eventual release. Our initiative accomplished that end at a much earlier date.

The pilgrimage to Damascus not only enlightened me, but it also enlightened a world smothered in the darkness of cynicism. Most importantly, for all believers, it strengthened our faith that the God we serve is not only symbol, but substance also. God was in the plan. The power of prayer in this pilgrimage was obvious. For a brief moment, the world seemed to be at a geo-political standstill. In the midst of that impasse, our faith action sent a message of reconciliation. Catholics prayed with Protestants, Blacks prayed with whites, Jews with Arabs; for too brief a moment, everyone gathered at the table of brotherhood linked by the commonality of prayer.

The Road to Damascus underscored the fact that there are seven continents but only one world. In this world we must learn to live together as friends or die apart as fools. As citizens of the world community, we have an obligation to make it safe for everyone, to insure equality for all human beings and to guarantee equal protection under the law for all people.

We must recognize, as did Martin Luther King Jr., that we need to develop a world-house; we must learn to appreciate that the world has become a global village where military resources cannot establish peace. We must opt for negotiation over against confrontation. America, heed the call! Peace is possible if we just give peace a chance.

Press List On Return to USA
Via Air Force 2

Anna Clopet	Newsweek photographer
Liz Colton	Newsweek reporter
Jack White	Time reporter
Tom Hartwell	Time photographer
Ken Walker	ABC-TV reporter
Michael Cheers	Jet photojournalist
Tracey Gray	WAOK (Atlanta) reporter
Rick Atkinson	Washington Post reporter
Kent Jarrett	CBS-TV producer
Bob Fane	CBS-TV reporter
Jamie Gangel	NBC-TV reporter
Matthew Quinn	UPI reporter
Rick Lipski	UPI photographer
Ron Smothers	N.Y. Times
Terry Anderson	AP reporter
Mervin Yates	NBC camera
Ken Guest	BBC-TV sound
Franklin Lamb	Freelance / Mid-East expert
Lee May	L.A. Times reporter

INDEX

INDEX (continued)

K

Khaddam, Abdel Halim 2, 3,
41, 42, 43, 44, 45, 46, 57,
64, 109, 110, 111, 113, 114,
123
Khan el Khalil 96
King, Martin Luther Jr. 3, 30,
31, 112, 134, 135
Knight, Carolyn Ann 8, 27, 78

L

Labadi, Mahmoud 80, 81, 82
Lagos, Nigeria 45
Lamb, Franklin 79
Lange, Mart T. 50
Lebanese National Front 46
Lebanon 69
Lipski, Rick 75

M

Maximy, Antoine de 75
Memphis 3, 7, 13, 28, 118
Mendelsohn, Jack 28, 42, 44,
74, 86, 109
Miller, Patrick 89, 105
Ministry of Religion and
Endowment 52, 53
Moody, Howard 10, 11 12
Moore, Bishop Paul 10, 11
Muhammad, Akbar 28, 99,
100, 126
Murphy, Richard 18, 20

N

National Council of Churches
54
NBC 92
New York Times 29, 133
Newsweek 29, 133

O

O'Brien, Pat 59, 105, 120
Old City, Jerusalem 96
Omayyad Mosque 97, 98

P

Paganelli, Robert, 20, 35, 77,
85, 113, 114, 115, 116, 117,
118, 123
Palestine National Council 47
Palestinian refugees 72
Peoples Market 96
Percy, Senator Charles 9, 127

Pinckney, Arnold 17
PLO 82
Porter, Thomas (Tom) 17, 20,
28, 30, 38, 41, 42, 44, 47,
63, 64, 74, 85, 96, 97, 101,
109, 110
Presbyterian Church 40
Presley, Elvis 5
Princeton Seminary 101
PUSH 6

Q

Queens College 40

R

Raad, Inaan 46, 65
Reagan Administration 18, 23
Republic of Syria 41, 110
Reuters 102, 104, 126
Rhein-Mainz 120
Riverside Church 10
Roman Catholic 54
Rugh, William 49, 51
Rumsfeld, Donald 5

S

Sabra 65
Saturday Night Live 92
Secret Service 1, 30, 32, 38,
39, 41, 46, 68, 81, 85, 87,
90, 91, 92, 95, 100, 104,
107, 116, 119
Shatilla 65
Sheraton-Damascus 37, 49
Shi'ite 54
Souk el-Hamideh 85, 96, 97,
98, 122
Smothers, Ronald 60
State Department 9, 14, 17,
18, 83, 120
Streathearn, Bruce 33, 38,
53, 77, 83, 85, 105
Street Called Straight 96
Sunni 54
Syrian Orthodox 54
Syrian Parliament 73
Syrian Political Security 70,
116, 119, 122

T

Tate, Florence 28, 38, 45, 46,
47, 48, 49, 63, 72, 75, 96,
101, 104, 111, 128

INDEX (continued)

Time Magazine 29, 75, 82
Theobald, Ed 28, 99, 100,
    101, 121
Thomas, Dr. Andrew 28, 38,
    41, 42
TWA 27

U
UPI 75
U.S. Embassy 115
U.S. Marines 113

V
Vivian, C.T. 7

W
Walker, Ann 8, 61
Walters, Dr. Ronald 17
Washington Post 5, 29
Wells, Dr. Aaron 25, 27
West Bank 69
Wheeler, Eugene 17, 30, 37,
    64, 100, 106, 121, 122
White Jack 60
Williams, Frederick Boyd 11
World Council of Churches 54
World Day of Prayer 76
World Peace Movement 30